Birds of Florida

Field Guide

by Stan Tekiela

ADVENTURE PUBLICATIONS, INC.
CAMBRIDGE, MINNESOTA

TO MY WIFE KATHERINE AND
DAUGHTER ABIGAIL WITH ALL MY LOVE

ACKNOWLEDGMENTS:

Special thanks to Tony Hertzel for range maps, and Florida birders Bill Pranty, who is on staff at Audubon of Florida, and Wes Biggs, President of Florida Nature Tours, for reviewing them. Special thanks also to Sandy Livoti for her exceptional eye to detail.

Book design and illustrations by Jonathan Norberg

Photo credits by photographer and page number:

Cover photo: Brian E. Small
Dominique Braud: 318 (adult) **Brian Collins**: 2, 142, 198, 274, 282 **Cornell Laboratory of Ornithology**: 86, 88 (female), 96 (perching), 148, 240 (both) **Dudley Edmondson**: 12, 14, 20, 24 (soaring), 64 (soaring), 66 (breeding), 68 (all), 92 (non-breeding adult, white juvenile), 98, 112 (both), 116, 122, 124, 136 (in flight), 144, 150 (both), 152 (male), 158, 164 (displaying), 170 (perching), 186 (both), 196, 202 (all), 210 (male), 216 (breeding), 224, 238 (male), 248 (perching, soaring), 250, 252, 254 (winter, displaying), 256, 296 (juvenile), 304 (breeding), 312 (breeding), 314 (adult), 322 (male, winter male), 324, 328 **Carrol Henderson**: 108 **Kevin T. Karlson**: 22 (soaring), 30 (male), 46, 48, 50, 56 (both), 62 (both), 128, 140 (female), 156, 218, 244, 246, 258 (juvenile), 302 (winter), 306 (breeding), 310, 326 **Bruce Leventhal**: 316 **Bill Marchel**: 4, 34 (male), 40, 88 (male), 102, 146, 166, 180, 182, 210 (female), 264, 266 (both), 276, 284, 290 **Maslowski Wildlife Productions**: 32, 84, 106, 120, 132, 204, 208, 226, 294, 318 (chick-feeding adult), 320, 332 **Arthur Morris**: 58, 140 (male) **Steve Mortensen**: 8, 34 (male), 36 (male), 38 (both), 60 (both), 64 (perching), 74, 78, 80 (both), 110, 188, 212, 222, 272, 322 (female) **Warren Nelson**: 10, 36 (female), 96 (soaring), 152 (female), 160 **John Pennoyer**: 100, 134, 190, 280, 288, 334 **Brian E. Small**: 18, 22 (perching), 26, 52, 66 (winter), 70, 72, 90, 126 (winter), 130, 162, 164 (breeding), 168, 172, 184, 194, 206, 216 (winter), 220, 228, 230, 234, 242, 258 (adult), 268 (both), 270, 286, 292, 302 (breeding), 304 (winter, juvenile), 306 (in flight), 312 (winter), 330 **Stan Tekiela**: 6 (both), 16, 28 (both), 30 (female, juvenile), 42 (both), 44 (breeding), 54, 76, 82 (both), 92 (breeding, molting female), 94, 104, 114, 118, 126 (breeding), 136 (perching), 138, 154, 174, 176, 178, 200, 214, 232, 236, 238 (female), 248 (juvenile), 260, 262, 278, 296 (adult), 298 (in flight), 300, 306 (winter), 308, 314 (juvenile) **Brian K. Wheeler**: 24 (perching), 170 (soaring) **Jim Zipp**: 44 (winter), 192, 298 (perching)

To the best of the publisher's knowledge, all photos except the female Indigo Bunting were of live birds.

TABLE OF CONTENTS

Introduction

Sample Page

The Birds

Helpful Resources

Check List/Index

About the Author

WHY WATCH BIRDS IN FLORIDA?

Millions of people have discovered bird feeding. It's a simple and enjoyable way to bring the beauty of birds closer to your home. Watching birds at your feeder often leads to a lifetime pursuit of bird identification. The *Birds of Florida Field Guide* is for those who want to identify common birds of Florida.

There are over 800 species of birds found in North America. In Florida alone there have been more than 480 different kinds of birds recorded through the years. That is an amazing amount of birds for one state! These bird sightings were diligently recorded by hundreds of bird watchers and became part of the official state record. From these valuable records, I have chosen 140 of the most common and easily seen birds of Florida to include in this field guide.

Bird watching, often called birding, is the largest spectator sport in America. Its outstanding popularity in Florida is due, in part, to an unusually rich and abundant bird life. Why are there so many birds in this state? One reason is water, both saltwater and fresh. Peninsular Florida is surrounded by water and has 1,350 miles (2,175 km) of coastline. It's home to many ocean-loving birds such as the colony-nesting Royal Tern and surf-running Sanderling. In addition to the coast, Florida has several hundred sizable lakes such as Lake Okeechobee–the third largest lake in the U.S.–thousands of freshwater and saltwater marshes, not to mention four major rivers. All of this water attracts millions of birds such as the Tricolored Heron and Roseate Spoonbill.

Climate is another reason why Florida has so many birds. The northern part of Florida is classified as humid subtropical, while southern Florida is considered tropical wet, more typical of Central America. The relative warm climate affords birds extra time to raise more than one brood per season, or to feed here unimpeded during severe winters elsewhere.

Southern Florida not only attracts people to its warm winter climate, it is also a winter home to hundreds of migratory bird species. From tiny birds, such as the Palm and Black-and-white Warblers, to the Ruddy Turnstone, an ornately colored shore-bird that nests in coastal Alaska, millions of birds pack into southern Florida each winter to feed in the state's nutrient waters and fertile forests.

While water and weather are good reasons for a vast abundance of birds in Florida, keep in mind the great size of the state. Florida is the twenty-second largest state, covering approximately 59,988 square miles (156,000 sq. km), over 35 percent of which is covered with forest. Florida's forests are home to such birds as the Chuck-will's-widow, whose calls throughout the night can be heard each spring and summer.

Florida is one of the best places in North America to see a wide array of birds. Whether witnessing a nesting colony of herons and egrets in the Everglades or welcoming back the wintering shorebirds, bird watchers enjoy variety and excitement in Florida as each season turns to the next.

OBSERVE WITH A STRATEGY; TIPS FOR IDENTIFYING BIRDS

Identifying birds isn't as difficult as you might think. By following a few basic strategies, you can increase your chances of successfully identifying most birds you see! One of the first and easiest things to do when you see a new bird is to note its color. (Also, since this book is organized by color, you will go right to that color section to find it.)

Next, note the size of the bird. A strategy to quickly estimate size is to select a small-, medium- and large-sized bird to use for reference. For example, most people are familiar with robins. A robin, measured from the tip of its bill to the tip of its tail, is 10 inches long. Using the robin as an example of a medium-sized bird, select two other birds, one smaller and one larger. Many people use a House Sparrow, at about 6 inches, and an American Crow, about 18 inches. When you see a bird that you don't know, you can quickly ask yourself, "Is it smaller than a robin, but larger than a sparrow?" When you look in your field guide to help identify your bird, you'll know it's roughly between 6 and 10 inches long. This will help narrow your choices.

Next, note the size, shape and color of the bill. Is it long, thin, pointed, short, thick, blunt, curved or straight? Seed-eating birds, such as Northern Cardinals, have bills that are thick and strong enough to crack even the toughest seeds. Birds that sip nectar, such as Ruby-throated Hummingbirds, need long thin bills to reach deep into flowers. Hawks and owls tear their prey with very sharp, curved bills. Sometimes, just noting the bill shape can help you decide if the bird is a woodpecker, finch, blackbird or bird of prey.

Next, take a look around and note the habitat in which you see the bird. Is it wading in a saltwater marsh? Walking along a riverbank or on the beach? Soaring in the sky? Is it perched high in the trees or hopping along the forest floor? Because of their preferences in diet and habitat, you'll usually see robins hopping on the ground, but not often eating the seeds at your feeder. Or you'll see a Blue Jay sitting on the branches of a tree, but not climbing headfirst down the trunk of a tree like the Brown-headed Nuthatch.

Noticing what a bird is eating will give you another clue to help you identify that bird. Feeding is a big part of any bird's life. Fully one-third of all bird activity revolves around searching for and catching food, or actually eating. While birds don't always follow all the rules of what we think they eat, you can make some general assumptions. Northern Flickers, for instance, feed upon ants and other insects, so you wouldn't expect to see them visiting a backyard bird feeder. Some birds, such as the Barn Swallow and the Tree Swallow, feed on flying insects, and spend hours swooping and diving to catch a meal.

Sometimes you can identify a bird by the way it perches. Body posture can help you differentiate between an American Crow and a Red-tailed Hawk. American Crows lean forward over their feet on a branch, while hawks perch in a vertical position. Look for this the next time you see a large unidentified bird in a tree.

Birds in flight are often difficult to identify, but noting the size and shape of the wing will help. A bird's wing size is in direct proportion to its body size, weight and type of flying. The shape of the wing determines if the bird flies fast and with precision, or slowly and less precisely. Birds such as House Finches, which flit around in thick tangles of branches, have short round wings. Birds that soar on warm updrafts of air, such as Turkey Vultures, have long broad wings. Barn Swallows have short pointed wings that slice through air, propelling their swift and accurate flight.

Some birds have unique flight patterns that aid in identification. American Goldfinches fly in a distinctive up-and-down pattern that makes it look as if they are riding a roller coaster.

While it's not easy to make these observations in the short time you often have to watch a "mystery bird," practicing these methods of identification will greatly expand your skills in birding. Also, seek the guidance of a more experienced birder who will help you improve your skills and answer questions on the spot.

BIRD BASICS

It's easier to identify birds and communicate about them if you know the names of the different parts of a bird. For instance, it's much easier to use the word "crest" to refer to the erect feathers on the head of a Northern Cardinal than trying to describe it.

The following illustration points out the basic parts of a bird. Because it's a composite of many birds, it should not be confused with any actual bird.

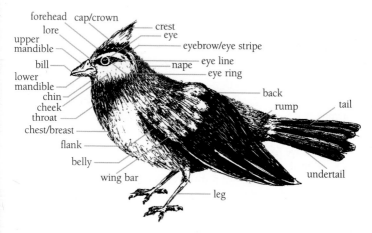

BIRD COLOR VARIABLES

No other animal has a color pallet like a bird's. Vivid blues, lemon yellows, intense reds and iridescent greens are commonplace within the bird world. In general, male birds are more colorful than their female counterparts. This is probably to help the male attract a mate, essentially saying, "Hey, look at me!" It also calls attention to the male's overall health. The better the condition of his feathers, the better his food source and territory, and therefore, the better his potential for a mate.

Females birds that don't look like their male counterparts (such species are called sexually dimorphic, meaning "two forms") are often a nondescript brown color, as seen with the Boat-tailed Grackle. These muted tones help to hide the females during weeks of motionless incubation, and draw less attention to her when she is out feeding or taking a break from the rigors of raising her young.

In some species, such as the Bald Eagle, Blue Jay and Downy Woodpecker, the male birds look nearly identical to the females. In the case of the woodpeckers, the sexes are only differentiated by a single red or sometimes yellow mark. Depending on the species, the mark may be on top of the head, face, nape of the neck or just behind the bill.

During the first year, juvenile birds often look like the mothers. Since brightly colored feathers are used mainly for attracting a mate, young non-breeding males don't have a need for colorful plumage. It is not until the first spring molt (or several years later, depending on the species) that young males obtain their breeding colors.

Both breeding and winter plumages are the result of molting. Molting is the process of dropping old worn feathers and replacing them with new ones. All birds molt, typically twice a year, with the spring molt usually occurring in late winter. During this time, most birds produce their breeding plumage (brighter colors for attracting mates), which lasts throughout the summer.

Winter plumage is the result of the late summer molt, which serves a couple of important functions. First, it adds feathers for warmth in the coming winter. Second, in some species it produces feathers that tend to be drab in color, which helps to camouflage the birds and hide them from predators. The winter plumage of the male American Goldfinch, for example, is an olive brown, unlike its obvious canary yellow color in summer. Luckily for us, some birds, such as the male Northern Cardinal, retain their bright summer colors all year long.

BIRD NESTS

Bird nests are truly an amazing feat of engineering. Imagine building your home strong enough to weather a storm, large enough to hold your entire family, insulated enough to shelter them from cold and heat, and waterproof enough to keep out rain. Now, build it without any blueprints or directions, and without the use of your hands or feet! Birds do!

Before building a nest, an appropriate site must be selected. With some birds, such as the House Wren, the male picks out several potential sites and assembles several small twigs in each. This discourages other birds from using nearby nest cavities. These "extra" nests are sometimes called dummy nests. The female is then taken around and shown all the choices. She chooses her favorite and finishes constructing the nest. With some other species of birds, for example, Baltimore Orioles, it's the female who chooses the site and builds the nest with the male only offering an occasional suggestion. Each bird species has its own nest-building routine, which is strictly followed.

Nesting material usually consists of natural elements found in the immediate area. Most nests consist of plant fibers (such as bark peeled from grapevines), sticks, feathers, mud, dried grass, feathers, fur, or the soft and fuzzy tufts from thistle. Some birds, including Ruby-throated Hummingbirds, use spider webs to glue their nest materials together. Nesting material is limited to what a bird can hold or carry. Because of this, a bird must make many trips afield to gather enough materials to complete its nest. Most nests take at least four days or more, and hundreds, if not thousands, of trips to build.

As you'll see in the following illustrations, birds build a wide variety of nest types.

ground nest   platform nest   cup nest   pendulous nest

The simple **ground nest** is scraped out of earth. These shallow depressions usually contain no nesting material, and are made by birds such as the Killdeer and Black Skimmer.

Another kind of nest, the **platform nest**, represents a more complex type of nest building. Constructed of small twigs and branches, the platform nest is a simple arrangement of sticks which forms a platform and features a small depression to nestle the eggs.

Some platform nests, such as those of the Common Loon, are constructed on the ground, and are made of mud and grass. Platform nests can also be on cliffs, bridges, balconies or even in flowerpots. This kind of nest gives space to adventurous youngsters, and functions as a landing platform for the parents. Many waterfowl construct platform nests on the ground, usually near water or actually in the water. These floating platform nests vary with the water level, thus preventing nests with eggs from being flooded. Platform nests, constructed by such birds as Mourning Doves and herons, are not anchored to the tree, and may tumble from the branches during high winds and storms.

The **cup nest** is a modified platform nest, used by three-quarters of all songbirds. Constructed from the outside in, a supporting platform is constructed first. This platform is attached firmly to a tree, shrub or rock ledge. Next, the sides are constructed of grasses, small twigs, bark or leaves, which are woven together and often glued with mud for additional strength. The inner cup, lined with feathers, animal fur, soft plant material or animal hair, is constructed last. The mother bird uses her chest to cast the final contours of the inner nest.

The **pendulous nest** is an unusual nest, looking more like a sock hanging from a branch than a nest. Inaccessible to most predators, these nests are attached to the ends of the smallest branches of a tree, and often wave wildly in the breeze. Woven very tightly of plant fibers, they are strong and watertight, taking up to a week to build. More commonly used by tropical birds, this complicated nest type has also been mastered by orioles and kinglets. A small opening on the top or side allows the parents access to the grass-lined interior. (It must be one heck of a ride to be inside one of these nests during a windy spring thunderstorm!)

One of the most clever of all nest types is known as the **no nest** or daycare nest. Parasitic birds, such as Brown-headed Cowbirds, build no nests at all! The egg-laden female expertly searches out other birds' nests and sneaks in to lay one of her own eggs while the host mother is not looking, thereby leaving the host mother to raise an adopted youngster. The mother cowbird wastes no energy building a nest only to have it raided by a predator. By using several nests of other birds, she spreads out her progeny in hope that at least one of her offspring will live to maturity.

Another nest type, the **cavity nest**, is used by many birds, including woodpeckers and Eastern Bluebirds. The cavity nest is usually excavated in a tree branch or trunk, and offers shelter from storms, cold, predators and the heat of Florida's climate. A relatively small entrance hole in a tree leads to an inner chamber up to 10 inches below. In some cases, a 4-foot tunnel connects the entrance in a riverbank to the nest chamber. These nests are often sparsely lined because they are well insulated. Usually constructed by woodpeckers and kingfishers, the cavity nest is used only once by its builder, but can be used for many years by birds such as mergansers, Tree Swallows and bluebirds, which do not have the capability of excavating one for themselves.

Some birds, including some swallows, take nest building one step further. They use a collection of small balls of mud to construct an adobe-style home. Constructed under the eaves of houses, under bridges or inside chimneys, some of these nests look like simple cup nests. Others are completely enclosed, with small tunnel-like openings that lead into a safe nesting chamber for the baby birds.

WHO BUILDS THE NEST?

In general, the female bird builds the nest. She gathers nesting materials and constructs a nest, with an occasional visit from her mate to check on the progress. In some species, both parents contribute equally to the construction of a nest. A male bird might forage for precisely the right sticks, grass or mud, but it's often the female that forms or puts together the nest. She uses her body to form the egg chamber. Rarely does the male build a nest by himself.

FLEDGING

Fledging is the interval between hatching and flight or leaving the nest. Some birds leave the nest within hours of hatching (precocial), but it might be weeks before they are able to fly. This is common with waterfowl and shorebirds. Until they start to fly, they are called fledglings. Birds that are still in the nest are called nestlings. Other baby birds are born naked and blind, and remain in the nest for several weeks (altricial).

WHY BIRDS MIGRATE

Why do birds migrate? The short answer is simple–food. Birds migrate to areas of high food concentrations. It is easier to breed where food is than where it is not. A typical migrating bird, the Summer Tanager, for instance, migrates from the tropics of Central and South America to nest in the forests of North America, taking advantage of billions of newly hatched insects to feed its young. This trip is called **complete migration**.

Some birds of prey return from their complete migration to northern regions that are overflowing with small rodents, such as mice and voles, that have continued to breed in winter.

Complete migrators have a set time and pattern of migration. Each year at nearly the same time, they take off and head for a specific wintering ground–often Florida. Complete migrators may travel incredible distances, sometimes as much as 15,000 miles or more in one year. But complete migration doesn't necessarily imply flying from the cold and frozen northland to a South American destination. The Baltimore Oriole, for example, is a complete migrator that flies from southern states which have mild winters, such as Tennessee and Mississippi, to spend the winter here in Florida. This is still called complete migration.

There are many interesting aspects to complete migrators. In the spring, males usually migrate several weeks before the females, arriving early to scope out possible nesting sites and food sources, and to begin to defend territories. The females arrive several weeks later. In the autumn, in many species, the females and their young leave early, often up to four weeks before the adult males.

Not all migrators are the same. There are **partial migrators**, such as American Goldfinches, that usually wait until food supplies dwindle before they migrate. Unlike complete migrators, the partial migrators move only far enough south, or sometimes east and west, to find abundant food. Some years it might be only a few hundred miles, while other years it might be nearly a thousand. This kind of migration, dependent upon the weather and available food, is sometimes called **seasonal movement**.

Unlike the predictable ebbing and flowing behavior of complete migrators or partial migrators, **irruptive migrators** can move every third to fifth year, or in some cases, in consecutive years. These irruptive migrations are triggered when times are really tough and food is scarce. Purple Finches are a good example of irruptive migrators, because they leave their normal northern range in search of food or in response to overpopulation.

How Do Birds Migrate?

One of the many secrets of migration is fat. While we humans are fighting the battle of the bulge, birds intentionally gorge themselves to put on as much fat as possible while still being able to fly. Fat provides the greatest amount of energy per unit of weight, and in the same way that your car needs gas, birds are propelled by fat or stalled without it.

During long migratory flights, fat deposits are used up quickly, and birds need to stop to "refuel." This is when backyard bird feeding stations and undeveloped, natural spaces around our towns and cities are especially important. Some birds require up to two to three days of constant feeding to build up their fat reserves before continuing their seasonal trip.

Some birds, such as most eagles, hawks, ospreys, falcons and vultures, migrate during the day. Larger birds can hold more body fat, go longer without eating and take longer to migrate. These birds glide along on rising columns of warm air, called thermals, which hold them aloft while they slowly make their way north or south. They generally rest at night and hunt early in the morning before the sun has a chance to warm up the land and create good soaring conditions. Birds migrating during the day use a combination of landforms, rivers and the setting sun to guide them in the right direction.

Most other birds migrate during the night. Studies show that some birds which migrate at night use the stars to navigate. Others use the setting sun, while still others, such as doves, use the earth's magnetic fields to guide them north or south. While flying at night might seem like a crazy idea, nocturnal migration is safer for several reasons. First, there are fewer nighttime predators for migrating birds. Second, traveling at night allows time during the day to find food in unfamiliar surroundings. Finally, nighttime wind patterns tend to be flat, or laminar. These flat winds don't have the turbulence associated with the daytime winds, and can actually help carry smaller birds by pushing them along.

HOW TO USE THIS GUIDE

To help you quickly and easily identify birds, this book is organized by color. Simply note the color of the bird and turn to that section. Refer to the first page for the color key. The Red-headed Woodpecker, for example, is black and white with a red head. Because the bird is mostly black and white, it will be found in the black and white section. Each color section is also arranged by size, generally with the smaller birds first. Sections may also incorporate the average size in a range, which in some cases reflects size differences between the male and female birds. Flip through the pages in that color section to find the bird. If you already know the name of the bird, check the index for the page number. In some species, the male and female are remarkably different in color. In others, the color of the breeding and winter plumages differs. These species have an inset photograph with a page reference and in most cases are found in two color sections.

In the description section you will find a variety of information about the bird. On the next page is a sample of the information included in the book.

RANGE MAPS

Range maps are included for each bird. Colored areas indicate where in Florida a particular bird is most likely to be found. Green is used for summer, blue for winter, red for year-round and yellow for areas where the bird is seen during migration. While every effort has been made to accurately depict these ranges, they are only general guidelines. Ranges actually change on an ongoing basis due to a variety of factors. Changes in weather, species abundance, landscape and vital resources such as the availability of food and water can affect local populations, migration and movements, causing birds to be found in areas not typical for the species.

Colored areas simply mean bird sightings for that species have been frequent in those areas and less frequent in the others. Please use the maps as intended–as general guides only.

COMMON NAME
Scientific name

COLOR INDICATOR

YEAR-ROUND
MIGRATION
SUMMER
WINTER

RANGE MAP

Size: measures head to tail, may include wingspan

Male: a brief description of the male bird, and may include breeding, winter or other plumages

Female: a brief description of the female bird, which is sometimes not the same as the male

Juvenile: a brief description of the juvenile bird, which often looks like the female

Nest: the kind of nest this bird builds to raise its young, who builds the nest, and how many broods per year

Eggs: how many eggs you might expect to see in a nest, and the color of the eggs

Incubation: the average time the parents spend incubating the eggs, and who does the incubation

Fledging: the average time the young spend in the nest after hatching but before they leave the nest, and which parent(s) does most of the "child-care" and feeding

Migration: type of migration: complete (consistent, seasonal), or partial (seasonal, destination varies), or irruptive (unpredictable, depending on the food supply), or non-migrator

Food: what the bird eats most of the time (e.g., seeds, nectar, insects, fruit, small animals), and if it typically comes to a bird feeding station

Compare: notes about other birds that look similar, and the pages on which they can be found

Stan's Notes: Interesting gee-whiz natural history information. This could be something to look or listen for, or something to help positively identify the bird. Also includes remarkable features.

female
pg. 121

male

YEAR-ROUND

EASTERN TOWHEE
Pipilo erythrophthalmus

Size: 7-8" (18-20 cm)

Male: A mostly black bird with dirty-red-brown sides and white belly. Long black tail with white tip. Short, stout, pointed bill. White wing patches flash in flight. Off-white eyes.

Female: similar to male, but is brown, not black

Juvenile: light brown, a heavily streaked head, chest and belly, long dark tail with white tip

Nest: cup; female builds; 2 broods per year

Eggs: 3-4; creamy white with brown markings

Incubation: 12-13 days; female incubates

Fledging: 10-12 days; female and male feed young

Migration: complete, to southern states and South America, winters in Florida

Food: insects, seeds, fruit, visits ground feeders

Compare: Slightly smaller than the American Robin (pg. 239). The Gray Catbird (pg. 233) lacks a black "hood" and rusty sides. Common Grackle (pg. 11) lacks white belly and has long thin bill.

Stan's Notes: Common name comes from its distinctive "tow-hee" call given by both sexes. Mostly known for its characteristic call that sounds like, "Drink-your-tea!" Seen hopping backward with both feet to rake up leaf litter (bilateral scratching), in search of insects and seeds. The female broods, but male does most of the feeding of young. White-eyed form in Florida.

female pg. 125

male

YEAR-ROUND

BROWN-HEADED COWBIRD
Molothrus ater

Size: 7½" (19 cm)

Male: A glossy black bird, reminiscent of a Red-winged Blackbird. Chocolate brown head with a pointed, sharp gray bill.

Female: dull brown bird with bill similar to male

Juvenile: similar to female, only dull gray color and a streaked chest

Nest: no nest; lays eggs in nests of other birds

Eggs: 5-7; white with brown markings

Incubation: 10-13 days; host bird incubates eggs

Fledging: 10-11 days; host birds feed young

Migration: complete, to southern states, winters in Florida

Food: insects, seeds, will come to seed feeders

Compare: In the blackbird family. The slightly larger male Red-winged Blackbird (pg. 9) has red and yellow markings on wings. Common Grackle (pg. 11) has a long tail and lacks the brown head. European Starling (pg. 7) has yellow bill and shorter tail.

Stan's Notes: Of about 750 species of parasitic birds worldwide, this is the only parasitic bird in Florida, laying all eggs in host birds' nests, leaving others to raise its young. Cowbirds are known to have laid eggs in nests of over 200 species of birds. Some birds reject cowbird eggs, but most raise them, even to the exclusion of their own young. Look for warblers and other birds feeding young birds twice their own size. At one time cowbirds followed bison to feed on the insects attracted to the animals.

winter

breeding

EUROPEAN STARLING
Sturnus vulgaris

YEAR-ROUND

Size: 7½" (19 cm)

Male: Iridescent purple black bird covered with white speckles during autumn and winter. Shiny purple black in spring and summer. Long, pointed yellow bill in the spring and gray in autumn. Short tail.

Female: same as male

Juvenile: similar to adult, only a gray brown with a streaked chest

Nest: cavity; male and female line the cavity; 2 broods per year

Eggs: 4-6; bluish with brown markings

Incubation: 12-14 days; female and male incubate

Fledging: 18-20 days; female and male feed young

Migration: non-migrator to partial migrator, some will move to southern states

Food: insects, seeds, fruit, comes to seed and suet feeders

Compare: Looks similar to Common Grackle (pg. 11), but lacks its long tail.

Stan's Notes: A great songster, it is also able to mimic sounds. Often displaces woodpeckers, chickadees and other cavity-nesting birds. Can be very aggressive and destroy eggs or young of other birds. The bill changes color with the seasons: yellow in spring and gray in autumn. Jaws are designed to be the most powerful when opening, as they pry open crevices to locate hidden insects. Gathers in the hundreds in autumn. Not a native bird, it was introduced to New York City in 1890-91 from Europe.

female pg. 135

male

RED-WINGED BLACKBIRD
Agelaius phoeniceus

YEAR-ROUND

Size: 8½" (22 cm)

Male: Jet black bird with red and yellow shoulder patches on upper wings. Pointed black bill.

Female: heavily streaked brown bird with a pointed brown bill and white eyebrows

Juvenile: same as female

Nest: cup; female builds; 2-3 broods per year

Eggs: 3-4; bluish green with brown markings

Incubation: 10-12 days; female incubates

Fledging: 11-14 days; female and male feed young

Migration: complete, to southern states, Mexico and Central America, winters in Florida

Food: seeds, insects, will come to seed feeders

Compare: Slightly larger than the male Brown-headed Cowbird (pg. 5), but is less iridescent and lacks Cowbird's brown head. Differs from all blackbirds due to the red and yellow patches on its wings (epaulets).

Stan's Notes: One of the most widespread and numerous birds in Florida. Each fall and winter, migrant and resident Red-wingeds gather in huge numbers (thousands) with other blackbirds to feed in agricultural fields, marshes and wetlands. Male defends territory by singing from the tops of surrounding vegetation. Repeats call from top of cattail while showing off its red and yellow wing bars (epaulets). The nest is usually over shallow water in a thick stand of cattails. Feeds mostly on seeds in spring and fall, switching to insects during summer. Female chooses mate.

COMMON GRACKLE
Quiscalus quiscula

YEAR-ROUND

Size: 11-13" (28-33 cm)

Male: Large black bird with iridescent blue black head, purple brown body, long black tail, long thin bill and bright golden eyes.

Female: similar to male, only duller and smaller

Juvenile: similar to female

Nest: cup; female builds; 2 broods per year

Eggs: 4-5; greenish white with brown markings

Incubation: 13-14 days; female incubates

Fledging: 16-20 days; female and male feed young

Migration: complete, to southern states, winters in Florida

Food: fruit, seeds, insects, comes to seed feeders

Compare: Male Boat-tailed Grackle (pg. 17) is slightly larger and has a much longer tail. European Starling (pg. 7) is much smaller and has a speckled appearance and yellow bill. Male Red-winged Blackbird (pg. 9) has red and yellow wing markings.

Stan's Notes: Usually nests in small colonies of up to 75 pairs, but travels with other blackbirds in large flocks. Is known to feed in farmers' fields. Name comes from the Latin word *graculus*, meaning "to cough," for its loud raspy call. Holds its tail in a keel-like position during flight. The flight pattern is almost always level, as opposed to having undulating up-and-down movements. Unlike most birds, has larger muscles to open mouth rather than to close it, as it pries open crevices to locate hidden insects. Not as common as the Boat-tailed Grackle.

11

COMMON MOORHEN
Gallinula chloropus

YEAR-ROUND

Size: 14" (36 cm)

Male: Nearly black overall with yellow-tipped red bill. Red forehead. Thin line of white along sides. Yellowish-green legs.

Female: same as male

Juvenile: same as adult, but brown with white throat, legs dirty yellow

Nest: ground; female and male build; 1-2 broods per year

Eggs: 2-10; brown with dark markings

Incubation: 19-22 days; female and male incubate

Fledging: 40-50 days; female and male feed young

Migration: complete, to Central and South America, winters in Florida

Food: insects, snails, seeds

Compare: Similar size as the American Coot (pg. 15), which lacks the distinctive yellow-tipped bill and red forehead of Moorhen. Similar size as the Purple Gallinule (pg. 91), which has an iridescent blue and green body.

Stan's Notes: Also known as Mud Hen or Pond Chicken. A nearly all-black duck-like bird often seen in freshwater marshes and lakes. Walks on floating vegetation or swims while hunting for insects. Females known to lay eggs in other moorhen nests in addition to their own. Sometimes takes old nest in a low shrub. A cooperative breeder, having young of first brood help raise young of second. Young leave nest usually within a few hours after hatching, but stay with the family for a couple months. Young ride on backs of adults.

YEAR-ROUND
WINTER

AMERICAN COOT
Fulica americana

Size: 13-16" (33-40 cm)

Male: Slate gray to black all over, white bill with dark band near tip. Green legs and feet. A small white patch near the base of the tail. Prominent red eyes and a small red patch above bill between eyes.

Female: same as male

Juvenile: much paler than adult, with a gray bill and same white rump patch

Nest: floating platform; female and male build; 1 brood per year

Eggs: 9-12; pinkish buff with brown markings

Incubation: 21-25 days; female and male incubate

Fledging: 49-52 days; female and male feed young

Migration: complete, to southern states and Central America, non-migrator in most of Florida

Food: insects, aquatic plants

Compare: Smaller than most waterfowl, it is the only black water bird or duck-like bird with a white bill.

Stan's Notes: An excellent diver and swimmer, often seen in large flocks on open water. Not a duck, as it doesn't have webbed feet, but instead has large lobed toes. When taking off, it scrambles across the surface of the water with wings flapping. Look for it to bob its head while swimming. Huge flocks of up to 1,000 birds gather for migration. The unusual name is of unknown origin, but in Middle English, the word *coote* was used to describe various waterfowl–perhaps it stuck. Nest is floating mat of vegetation.

female pg. 163

male

BOAT-TAILED GRACKLE
Quiscalus major

YEAR-ROUND

Size:	16" (40 cm), male 14" (36 cm), female
Male:	Iridescent blue-black bird with a very long keel-shaped tail. Brown or yellow eyes.
Female:	brown version of male, lacks iridescence
Juvenile:	similar to adult
Nest:	cup; female builds; 2 broods per year
Eggs:	2-4; pale greenish blue, brown markings
Incubation:	13-15 days; female incubates
Fledging:	12-15 days; female feeds young
Migration:	non-migrator, moves around to find food
Food:	insects, berries, seeds, fish, visits feeders
Compare:	Similar to male Common Grackle (pg. 11), but male Boat-tailed has a distinctive long tail. Similar size as both species of Crow (pp. 19 and 21), but a very different shape. Look for an iridescent blue head and a very long tail.

Stan's Notes: A bird of coastal saltwater and inland marshes. Boat-taileds north of Gainesville have yellow eyes, but in the rest of Florida the birds have brown eyes. A noisy bird that gives several harsh, high-pitched calls and several squeaks. Eats a wide variety of foods from grains to fish. Sometimes seen picking insects off the backs of cattle. Will also visit bird feeders. Makes a cup nest with mud or cow dung and grass. Nests in small colonies. Most nesting occurs from February through July and occasionally again from October to December.

FISH CROW
Corvus ossifragus

YEAR-ROUND

Size: 16" (40 cm)

Male: All-black bird appearing nearly identical to the American Crow, but with a longer tail, and smaller head and bill.

Female: same as male

Juvenile: same as adult

Nest: cup; female and male build; 1 brood a year

Eggs: 4-5; blue or gray-green, brown markings

Incubation: 16-18 days; female and male incubate

Fledging: 21-24 days; female and male feed young

Migration: non-migrator

Food: aquatic insects, carrion, mollusks, berries, seeds

Compare: Nearly identical to American Crow (pg. 21), but the Fish Crow is smaller, has a longer tail, and a smaller head and bill. Fish Crow is most easily differentiated by its higher pitched call.

Stan's Notes: Essentially a bird of the coastal tidewaters and along major rivers, but can be found throughout the state. Not uncommon for it to break open mollusk shells by dropping onto rocks from above. Very sociable and gregarious. Nests in small colonies, often building a stick nest halfway up a tree. Forms small winter flocks of up to 100 birds, unlike the American Crow, which often forms winter flocks of several hundred. The best way to distinguish between the two crow species is by their remarkably different calls. The Fish Crow has a high, nasal "cah."

19

AMERICAN CROW
Corvus brachyrhynchos

YEAR-ROUND

Size: 18" (45 cm)

Male: All-black bird with black bill, legs and feet. Can have purple sheen in direct sunlight.

Female: same as male

Juvenile: same as adult

Nest: platform; female builds; 1 brood per year

Eggs: 4-6; bluish to olive green, brown markings

Incubation: 18 days; female incubates

Fledging: 28-35 days; female and male feed young

Migration: non-migrator to partial migrator

Food: fruit, insects, mammals, fish, carrion, will come to seed and suet feeders

Compare: Nearly identical to the Fish Crow (pg. 19), but American Crow is larger, has a shorter tail, and a larger head and bill. American Crow is most easily differentiated by its lower pitched call.

Stan's Notes: One of the most recognizable birds in Florida. Often reuses nest every year if not taken over by a Great Horned Owl. Collects and stores bright, shiny objects in the nest. Able to mimic human voices, and other birds. One of the smartest of all birds, it is very social, often entertaining itself by provoking chases with other birds. Feeds on road kill but is rarely hit by cars. Can live up to 20 years. Unmated birds, known as helpers, help raise young. Large extended families roost together at night, dispersing during the day to hunt.

soaring

BLACK VULTURE
Coragyps atratus

YEAR-ROUND

Size: 25" (63 cm); up to 4¾-foot wingspan

Male: Black vulture with dark gray head and legs. Short tail. In flight, all black with light-gray wing tips, and feet extending beyond tail.

Female: same as male

Juvenile: similar to adult

Nest: no nest on a stump or on ground, or takes abandoned nest; 1 brood per year

Eggs: 2; light green with dark markings

Incubation: 37-48 days; female and male incubate

Fledging: 80-90 days; female and male feed young

Migration: non-migrator

Food: dead animals, occasionally captures small live mammals

Compare: Slightly smaller than the Turkey Vulture (pg. 25), lacking Turkey Vulture's bright red head. Turkey Vulture has two-toned wings, a black leading edge and light-gray trailing edge. Black Vulture has shorter wings and tail than the Turkey Vulture.

Stan's Notes: Also called Black Buzzard. A more gregarious bird than the Turkey Vulture. In flight, the Black Vulture holds its wings straight out to its sides, unlike the Turkey Vulture which holds its wings in a V pattern. More aggressive while feeding but less skilled at finding carrion, it is thought Black Vulture's sense of smell is less developed than Turkey Vulture's. Families stay together for up to a year. Often nests and roosts with other Black Vultures. If startled, especially at the nest, it regurgitates with power and accuracy.

23

soaring

TURKEY VULTURE
Cathartes aura

Size: 26-32" (66-80 cm); up to 6-foot wingspan

Male: Large bird with obvious red head and legs. In flight, the wings appear two-toned: black leading edge with gray on the trailing edge and tip. The tips of wings end in finger-like projections. Squared-off tail. Ivory bill.

Female: same as male

Juvenile: same as adult, but often a gray-to-blackish head and bill

Nest: no nest, or minimal nest on cliff or in cave

Eggs: 2; white with brown markings

Incubation: 38-41 days; female and male incubate

Fledging: 66-88 days; female and male feed young

Migration: complete, to southern states, Central and South America, winters in Florida

Food: carrion, just about any dead animal of any size, parents regurgitate for young

Compare: Slightly larger than Black Vulture (pg. 23), and has longer wings and tail. Flies holding wings in a slight V shape, unlike the Black Vulture's straight wing position.

Stan's Notes: The Vulture's naked head is an adaptation to reduce the risk of feather fouling (picking up diseases) from carcasses. Unlike hawks and eagles, it has weak feet more suited to walking than grasping. One of the few birds with a developed sense of smell. Generally mute, it makes only grunts or groans. Groups often seen in trees with wings outstretched to catch sun.

YEAR-ROUND

MUSCOVY DUCK
Cairina moschata

Size: 28" (71 cm)

Male: Wide range of color patterns from a glossy green-black to all white, with some being black and white (pied). Large bumpy patch of flesh, often red, around eyes and base of bill. Usually has a white wing patch, seen when perched and in flight.

Female: smaller than male, lacking the bumpy skin patch

Juvenile: same as adult, lacking skin patch and white wing patch

Nest: ground; female builds; 1 brood per year

Eggs: 5-10; off-white without markings

Incubation: 25-27 days; female incubates

Fledging: 60-70 days; female shows the young what to eat

Migration: non-migrator

Food: aquatic insects, grass, seeds

Compare: Highly variable-colored duck that is easily identified by the bumpy skin patch around eyes and base of bill.

Stan's Notes: A year-round Florida resident. Naturally occurring in Central and South America, it is a non-native duck that has been released in urban parks, ponds and lakes. Nests at base of trees and roosts in trees at night, like Wood Ducks. Not uncommon to nest near human dwellings under shrubbery. Can be very aggressive.

drying

DOUBLE-CRESTED CORMORANT
Phalacrocorax auritus

YEAR-ROUND
MIGRATION

Size: 33" (83 cm)

Male: Large all-black water bird with long snake-like neck. A long yellow orange bill with a hooked tip.

Female: same as male

Juvenile: lighter brown with a grayish-colored breast and neck

Nest: platform, in colony; male and female build; 1 brood per year

Eggs: 3-4; bluish white, unmarked

Incubation: 25-29 days; female and male incubate

Fledging: 37-42 days; male and female feed young

Migration: complete, to southern states, Mexico and Central America, winters in most of Florida

Food: small fish, aquatic insects

Compare: Male Anhinga (pg. 31) is slightly larger with white spots and streaks, and a long straight bill without a hooked tip, like Cormorant. Similar size as the Turkey Vulture (pg. 25), which also perches with wings open to dry in sun, but lacks Vulture's naked red head.

Stan's Notes: Often seen flying in large V formation. Often roosts in large groups in trees near water. Catches fish by swimming with wings held at its sides. To dry off it strikes an erect pose with wings outstretched, facing the sun. The name refers to its nearly invisible crests. "Cormorant" comes from the Latin word *corvus*, meaning "crow," and *L. marinus*, meaning "pertaining to the sea," literally, "Sea Crow."

female

juvenile

male

ANHINGA
Anhinga anhinga

YEAR-ROUND

Size: 35" (88 cm); up to 3¾-foot wingspan

Male: All black with glossy green and white spots and streaks on shoulders and wings. Long neck and tail. Long, narrow yellow bill.

Female: similar to male, but has buff brown neck and breast

Juvenile: similar to adult, light-brown-to-white body

Nest: platform; female and male build; 1 brood per year

Eggs: 2-4; light blue without markings

Incubation: 26-29 days; female and male incubate

Fledging: 21-25 days; female and male feed young

Migration: non-migrator

Food: fish, aquatic insects, crustaceans and small mammals

Compare: The Double-crested Cormorant (pg. 29) is slightly smaller, and lacks white spots and streaks of male Anhinga. Cormorant has a shorter bill with curved tip, compared with the long straight bill of the Anhinga.

Stan's Notes: Also called Snakebird due to its habit of appearing like a snake—surfacing with just its head and long thin neck showing above the water. It skewers fish, a favorite prey, with its long sharp bill. Unlike ducks and other diving birds, its feathers become waterlogged, which helps diving and maneuvering underwater. Afterward, it often strikes a pose with wings spread to dry in the sun. A strong flyer, often seen soaring, and is confused with birds of prey. In flight, the long neck and tail help to identify.

BLACK-AND-WHITE WARBLER
Mniotilta varia

MIGRATION
WINTER

Size: 5" (13 cm)

Male: Striped like a zebra, this small warbler has a distinctive black-and-white striped cap. White belly. Black chin and cheek patch.

Female: same as male, only duller and without the black chin and cheek patch

Juvenile: brown version of adult

Nest: cup; female builds; 1 brood per year

Eggs: 4-5; white with brown markings

Incubation: 10-11 days; female incubates

Fledging: 9-12 days; female and male feed young

Migration: complete, to Florida, Central America and South America

Food: insects

Compare: Look for Black-and-white Warbler creeping down a tree trunk, like the Brown-headed Nuthatch (pg. 207).

Stan's Notes: One of the first warblers to arrive each fall, it is the only warbler that moves headfirst down a tree trunk. Look for this common warbler searching for insect eggs in the bark of large trees. Song sounds like a slowly turning, squeaky wheel. The female will perform a distraction dance to draw predators away from the nest. Makes its nest on the ground, concealed under dead leaves or at the base of a tree. Fall migrants arrive in August and depart in May. Found throughout the winter in a variety of habitats. Doesn't nest in Florida.

male

female

DOWNY WOODPECKER
Picoides pubescens

YEAR-ROUND

Size: 6" (15 cm)

Male: A small woodpecker with an all-white belly, black-and-white spotted wings, a black line running through its eyes, a short black bill, a white stripe down back and a red mark on nape of neck. Several small black spots along side of white tail.

Female: same as male, lacking red mark on nape

Juvenile: same as female, some juveniles can have a red mark near forehead

Nest: cavity; male and female excavate; 1 brood per year

Eggs: 3-5; white, unmarked

Incubation: 11-12 days; female and male incubate, the female during day, male at night

Fledging: 20-25 days; male and female feed young

Migration: non-migrator

Food: insects, seeds, visits seed and suet feeders

Compare: Almost identical to the Hairy Woodpecker (pg. 39), but smaller. Look for the shorter, thinner bill of Downy to differentiate them.

Stan's Notes: One of the most abundant woodpeckers. Both sexes will drum on a hollow log or branch to announce territories. Males perform most brooding and incubate all night. Small percentage of young will have a red spot on crown. Stiff tail feathers help brace the bird like a tripod as it clings to a tree branch. All woodpeckers have long barbed tongues, used to pull insects out of tiny places. Will winter roost in cavity.

male

female

YELLOW-BELLIED SAPSUCKER
Sphyrapicus varius

WINTER

Size: 8-9" (20-22.5 cm)

Male: Medium-sized woodpecker with checkered back. Has a red forehead, crown and chin. Tan-to-yellow chest and belly. White wing patches flash while flying.

Female: similar to male, white marking on chin

Juvenile: similar to adult, dull brown and lacks any red marking

Nest: cavity; female and male excavate; 1 brood per year

Eggs: 5-6; white, unmarked

Incubation: 12-13 days; female and male incubate, the female during day, male at night

Fledging: 25-29 days; female and male feed young

Migration: complete, to Florida, Central America and Mexico

Food: insects, tree sap

Compare: Similar to other woodpeckers, but the male is the only Florida woodpecker with a red chin patch. Female has white chin.

Stan's Notes: Drills holes in a pattern of horizontal rows in small- to medium-sized trees to bleed tree sap. Many birds drink from sapsucker taps. Oozing sap also attracts insects, which sapsuckers eat. Sapsuckers will defend their sapping sites from other birds. They don't suck sap; rather, they lap it with their long tongues. A quiet bird with few vocalizations, but will mew like a cat. Unlike other woodpeckers, drumming rhythm is irregular.

male

female

YEAR-ROUND

HAIRY WOODPECKER
Picoides villosus

Size: 9" (22.5 cm)

Male: Black-and-white woodpecker with a white belly and black wings with rows of white spots. White stripe down back. Long black bill. Red mark on back of head.

Female: same as male, lacks red spot

Juvenile: grayer version of adult, lacks red spot

Nest: cavity; female and male excavate; 1 brood per year

Eggs: 3-6; white, unmarked

Incubation: 11-15 days; female and male incubate, the female during day, male at night

Fledging: 28-30 days; male and female feed young

Migration: non-migrator.

Food: insects, nuts, seeds, comes to seed and suet feeders

Compare: Larger than Downy Woodpecker (pg. 35), Hairy has a longer bill and lacks Downy's black spots along tail.

Stan's Notes: A backyard bird that announces its arrival with a sharp chirp before landing on feeders. Barbed tongue helps extract insects from trees. Responsible for eating many destructive forest insects. Has tiny bristle-like feathers at the base of bill to protect nostrils from wood dust. Will drum on hollow logs, branches or stovepipes in spring to announce territory. Often prefers to excavate nest cavities in live trees. Has a larger, more oval-shaped cavity entrance than that of Downy Woodpecker.

YEAR-ROUND

RED-HEADED WOODPECKER
Melanerpes erythrocephalus

Size: 9" (22.5 cm)

Male: All-red head and a solid black back. White rump, chest and belly. Large white patches on wings flash when in flight. A black tail. Gray legs and bill.

Female: same as male

Juvenile: gray brown with white chest, lacks any red

Nest: cavity; male builds with help from female; 1 brood per year

Eggs: 4-5; white, unmarked

Incubation: 12-13 days; female and male incubate

Fledging: 27-30 days; female and male feed young

Migration: partial migrator, will move around to areas with abundant supply of nuts

Food: insects, nuts, fruit, comes to seed and suet feeders

Compare: No other woodpecker in Florida has an all-red head. Pileated Woodpecker (pg. 61) is the only other woodpecker that has a solid black back, but has a partial red head.

Stan's Notes: One of the few woodpecker species in which male and female appear the same (look alike). Bill is not as well adapted for excavating holes as in other woodpeckers, so it chooses dead or rotten tree branches for nest. Later nesting than the closely related Red-bellied Woodpecker and will often take over its nesting cavity. Prefers more open or edge woodland with many dead trees. Often seen perching on tops of dead snags. Stores acorns and other nuts.

male

female

RED-BELLIED WOODPECKER
Melanerpes carolinus

YEAR-ROUND

Size: 9¼" (23 cm)

Male: "Zebra-backed" woodpecker with a white rump. Red crown extends down the nape of neck. Tan breast with a tinge of red on belly, which is often hard to see.

Female: same as male, but gray crown

Juvenile: gray version of adult, no red crown or nape

Nest: cavity; the female and male build; 1 brood per year

Eggs: 4-5; white, unmarked

Incubation: 12-14 days; female and male incubate, the female during day, male at night

Fledging: 24-27 days; female and male feed young

Migration: non-migrator

Food: insects, nuts, fruit, comes to seed and suet feeders

Compare: Similar to Northern Flicker (pg. 153) and Yellow-bellied Sapsucker (pg. 37). Note the tan chest and belly with obvious black-and-white stripes on back. The male is the only woodpecker in the state with a red crown extending down the neck.

Stan's Notes: Named for its easily overlooked rosy-red belly patch. Probably the most widespread woodpecker in the state. Found in suburban yards to heavily forested areas. Excavates holes in rotten wood, looking for spiders, beetles and centipedes. Hammers acorns and berries into crevices of trees for winter food. Will return to same tree to excavate a new nest below that of previous year.

winter

breeding

WINTER

RUDDY TURNSTONE
Arenaria interpres

Size: 9½" (24 cm)

Male: Orange legs. A slightly upturned black bill. Breeding has a black and white head marking, black bib, white chest and belly, black and chestnut wings and back. Winter has a brown and white head and chest pattern.

Female: similar to male, only duller

Juvenile: similar to adult, but black and white head has a scaly appearance

Nest: ground; female builds; 1 brood per year

Eggs: 3-4; olive green with dark markings

Incubation: 22-24 days; male and female incubate

Fledging: 19-21 days; male feeds young

Migration: complete, to coastal Florida, South America

Food: aquatic insects, fish, mollusks, crustaceans, worms, eggs

Compare: Unusually ornamented shorebird. Look for a striking black and white pattern on head and neck, and orange legs to identify.

Stan's Notes: A common migrant and winter resident. Also called Rock Plover. Named "Turnstone" because it turns stones over on rocky beaches to find insects, worms and tiny creatures. Known for its unusual behavior of robbing and eating other birds' eggs. Will hang around crabbing operations to feed on scraps cleaned from nets. Can be very tolerant of humans when feeding. Females often leave before the young leave nests (fledge), resulting in the males raising young. Males have a bare spot on the belly (brood patch) to warm the young, something only females normally have.

winter pg. 247

breeding

MIGRATION
WINTER

BLACK-BELLIED PLOVER
Pluvialis squatarola

Size: 11-12" (28-30 cm)

Male: Black legs and bill. Striking black and white breeding plumage. Black belly, face, neck, chest and sides. A white cap, nape of neck and belly near tail.

Female: less black on chest and belly than male

Juvenile: grayer than adult, with much less black

Nest: ground; the male and female build; 1 brood per year

Eggs: 3-4; pinkish or greenish with black-brown markings

Incubation: 26-27 days; male and female incubate, the male during day, female at night

Fledging: 35-45 days; male feeds young, young learn quickly to feed themselves

Migration: complete, to the West Indies, East and Gulf coasts, coastal South America

Food: insects

Compare: The breeding Dunlin (pg. 131) is slightly smaller with a rusty back and long down-curved bill. Look for extensive black patch on belly, face and chest, and a white cap.

Stan's Notes: The males perform a "butterfly" courtship flight to attract females. Female leaves male and young about 12 days after the eggs hatch. Breeds at 3 years of age. Arrivals start in July and August (fall migration). In flight, in any plumage, Plover displays a white rump and stripe on the wings with black axillaries (armpits). Often darts across ground to grab an insect and run.

BLACK-NECKED STILT
Himantopus mexicanus

YEAR-ROUND
MIGRATION

Size: 14" (36 cm)

Male: Upper parts of the head, neck and back are black. Lower parts are white. Ridiculously long red-to-pink legs. Long black bill.

Female: similar to male, only browner on back

Juvenile: similar to adult, but brown instead of black

Nest: ground; the female and male build; 1 brood per year

Eggs: 3-5; off-white with dark markings

Incubation: 22-26 days; female and male incubate

Fledging: 28-32 days; female and male feed young

Migration: complete, to South America, non-migrator in southern Florida

Food: aquatic insects

Compare: Outrageous length of the red-to-pink legs make this shorebird hard to confuse with any other.

Stan's Notes: Although a year-round resident in southern Florida, it can be found along the East coast and as far north as the Great Lakes. Usually leaves northern Florida during winter, but a few remain. It is a common bird of shallow freshwater and saltwater marshes, and a very vocal bird, giving a "kek-kek-kek" call. Will nest solitarily or in small colonies in open areas above the tide line. Known to transport water with water-soaked belly feathers (belly-soaking) to cool eggs during hot weather.

female pg. 169

male

LESSER SCAUP
Aythya affinis

WINTER

Size: 16-17" (40-43 cm)

Male: Appears mostly black with bold white sides and gray back. Chest and head look nearly black, but head appears purple with green highlights in direct sun. Bright yellow eyes.

Female: overall brown with dull white patch at base of light-gray bill, yellow eyes

Juvenile: same as female

Nest: ground; female builds; 1 brood per year

Eggs: 8-14; olive buff without markings

Incubation: 22-28 days; female incubates

Fledging: 45-50 days; female teaches young to feed

Migration: complete, southern states, northern South America, Central America

Food: aquatic plants and insects

Compare: The male Ring-necked Duck (pg. 53) has a bold white ring around its bill and a black back, compared with male Lesser Scaup's gray back. Male Ring-necked lacks the bold white sides of the male Lesser Scaup.

Stan's Notes: A common diving duck in the state. Often seen in large flocks numbering in the thousands on area lakes, ponds and sewage lagoons. Mostly seen during migrations in late February and in October. When seen in flight, note the bold white stripe under the wings. Has an interesting baby-sitting arrangement in which the young form groups tended by one to three adult females.

female pg. 173

male

WINTER

RING-NECKED DUCK
Aythya collaris

Size: 17" (43 cm)

Male: A striking duck with black head, chest and back. Sides are gray to nearly white. Has a bold white ring around bill and a second ring at base of bill. Top of head is peaked.

Female: dark brown back, light brown sides, a gray face, dark brown crown, white line behind eyes and white ring around the bill, top of head peaked

Juvenile: similar to adult

Nest: ground; female builds; 1 brood per year

Eggs: 8-10; olive gray to brown, unmarked

Incubation: 26-27 days; female incubates

Fledging: 49-56 days; female teaches young to feed

Migration: complete, to southern states, West Indies, Central America

Food: aquatic plants and insects

Compare: Similar size as male Lesser Scaup (pg. 51), which has a gray back, compared with the black back of the male Ring-necked Duck. Look for the male Ring-necked's prominent white ring around the bill.

Stan's Notes: One of the most abundant wintering ducks in the state. Usually seen in larger freshwater lakes rather than saltwater marshes. A diving duck, watch for it to dive underwater to forage for food. Takes to flight by springing up off water. Named "Ring-necked" due to a cinnamon-colored collar (nearly impossible to see in the field). Also known as Ring-billed Duck.

female pg. 175

male

YEAR-ROUND
WINTER

HOODED MERGANSER
Lophodytes cucullatus

Size: 16-19" (40-48 cm)

Male: A sleek black-and-white bird with rusty brown sides. Crest "hood" raises to reveal large white patch. Long, thin black bill.

Female: sleek brown and rust bird with a ragged rusty crest and long, thin brown bill

Juvenile: similar to female

Nest: cavity; female lines old woodpecker hole; 1 brood per year

Eggs: 10-12; white, unmarked

Incubation: 32-33 days; female incubates

Fledging: 71 days; female feeds young

Migration: complete, to Gulf coast and Mexico, non-migrator in central Florida

Food: small fish, aquatic insects

Compare: A distinctive diving bird, look for the large white patch "hood" on the head and rusty sides. Similar size as the male Wood Duck (pg. 273), but lacking the green head of the Wood Duck.

Stan's Notes: A small diving bird of shallow-water ponds, sloughs, lakes and rivers. Rarely found away from wooded areas, where it nests in natural cavities or nest boxes. The male Hooded Merganser can voluntarily raise and lower its crest to show off the large white patch on its head. The female will "dump" eggs into other female Hooded Merganser nests, resulting in 20 to 25 eggs in some nests. Mergansers have been known to share a nesting cavity with Wood Ducks sitting side by side.

skimming

BLACK SKIMMER
Rynchops niger

YEAR-ROUND
MIGRATION
WINTER

Size: 18" (45 cm); up to 3½-foot wingspan

Male: A striking black and white bird with black on top and white on bottom. Very distinct black-tipped red bill with lower bill longer than the upper. Red legs tuck up and out of sight when in flight.

Female: similar to male, only smaller

Juvenile: similar to adult, spotty brown on top

Nest: ground; the female and male build; 1 brood per year

Eggs: 3-5; bluish-white with brown markings

Incubation: 21-23 days; female and male incubate

Fledging: 23-25 days; female and male feed young

Migration: complete, to South America, non-migrator in coastal Florida

Food: small fish, shrimp

Compare: Similar shape as Royal Tern (pg. 307), but lacks the black back and black-tipped red bill of Black Skimmer. No other large black and white bird skims across the water like Black Skimmer. In addition, no other bird with a lower bill longer than the upper bill.

Stan's Notes: Also called Scissorbill or Razorbill, referring to this bird's unusual, long bill. Uses its unique bill while in flight to cut through the water surface to catch fish or shrimp near the surface. Commonly feeds with several other skimmers. Often seen flying to and from nesting colony with fish in its bill. Nests in large colonies, often associated with tern species. Found up the East coast.

AMERICAN OYSTERCATCHER
Haematopus palliatus

YEAR-ROUND

Size: 18-19" (45-48 cm)

Male: A large shorebird with large red-orange bill, black head, and dark brown sides, wings and back. White chest and belly, pink legs and a red ring around the eyes.

Female: same as male

Juvenile: more gray than black and lacks the brightly colored bill

Nest: ground; the male and female build; 1 brood per year

Eggs: 2-4; olive with sparse brown markings

Incubation: 24-29 days; male and female incubate, the male during day, female at night

Fledging: 35-40 days; male and female feed young, young learn quickly to feed themselves

Migration: complete, to West Indies and East, Gulf and South American coasts, winters in Florida

Food: shellfish, insects, aquatic insects, worms

Compare: Larger than breeding Black-bellied Plover (pg. 47). Look for the large and obvious red-orange bill of Oystercatcher to identify.

Stan's Notes: A large, chunky shorebird with a flattened, heavy bill, used to pry open shellfish and to probe in the sand for insects and worms. Can be categorized according to its preferred oyster-opening technique. Stabbers sneak up on mollusks and stab their bills between shells before they have a chance to close. Hammerers shatter one-half of the shell with several direct, powerful blows.

male

female

PILEATED WOODPECKER
Dryocopus pileatus

YEAR-ROUND

Size: 19" (48 cm)

Male: Crow-sized woodpecker with a black back and bright red crest. Long gray bill with red mustache. White leading edge of the wings flashes brightly when flying.

Female: same as male, but has a black forehead and lacks red mustache

Juvenile: similar to adult, only duller and browner overall

Nest: cavity; male and female excavate; 1 brood per year

Eggs: 3-5; white, unmarked

Incubation: 15-18 days; female and male incubate, the female during day, male at night

Fledging: 26-28 days; female and male feed young

Migration: non-migrator

Food: insects, will come to suet feeders

Compare: Red-headed Woodpecker (pg. 41) is about half the size, and has an all-red head, black back and white rump.

Stan's Notes: Our largest woodpecker, it excavates long oval holes up to several feet long in tree trunks, searching for insects. Large chips of wood lay at the base of excavated trees. Will drum on hollow branches, chimneys, etc., to announce its territory. Relatively shy bird that prefers large tracts of woodland. The young are fed regurgitated insects. Favorite food is carpenter ants.

in flight

SWALLOW-TAILED KITE
Elanoides forficatus

Size: 23" (58 cm); up to 4-foot wingspan

Male: A white head, chest and belly. Black back, wings and tail. In flight, white leading edge of narrow pointed wings, a black trailing edge and a long, deeply forked tail. In the right light, black back and wings appear metallic green-blue.

Female: same as male

Juvenile: same as adult, but has a shorter tail

Nest: platform; female and male build; 1 brood per year

Eggs: 2-4; white with dark markings

Incubation: 26-28 days; female and male incubate

Fledging: 36-42 days; female and male feed young

Migration: complete, to Central and South America

Food: insects, snakes, lizards, frogs, mammals

Compare: Slightly smaller than the Osprey (pg. 65), which shares its black and white pattern. No other bird of prey in Florida has such a deeply forked tail.

Stan's Notes: A stunning bird in flight, where its contrasting black and white pattern and forked tail easily identify it. Feeds while in flight. Also drinks on the wing, skimming across the surface of the water like a swallow. Rarely seen hovering like other birds of prey. A very agile flyer, will collect sticks for nest like Ospreys by breaking off sticks with its feet as it flies. Semi-social, with a couple birds sharing the same territory. Prefers open woods and river bottoms. Found mostly in Florida, range was once as far north as Minnesota.

soaring

OSPREY
Pandion haliaetus

YEAR-ROUND

Size: 24" (60 cm); up to 6-foot wingspan

Male: Large eagle-like bird with white chest, belly and black brown back. White head with a black streak across eyes. Large wings with black "wrist" marks.

Female: same as male, but with a necklace of brown streaking

Juvenile: same as adult

Nest: platform; female and male build; 1 brood per year

Eggs: 2-4; white with brown markings

Incubation: 32-42 days; female and male incubate

Fledging: 48-58 days; male and female feed young

Migration: complete, to Mexico, Central America and South America, winters in Florida

Food: fish

Compare: Bald Eagle (pg. 69) is on average 10 inches larger, and has an all-white head and tail. The juvenile Bald Eagle is brown with white speckles. Look for a white belly and dark stripe across eyes to identify the Osprey.

Stan's Notes: Ospreys are in a family all their own. It is the only raptor that will plunge into the water to catch fish. Can hover for a few seconds before diving. Carries fish in a head-first position during flight for better aerodynamics. In flight, wings are angled (cocked) backward. Nests on man-made towers and tall dead trees. Recent studies show that male and female might mate for life, but don't migrate to the same wintering grounds.

winter

breeding

COMMON LOON
Gavia immer

MIGRATION
WINTER

Size: 28-36" (71-90 cm)

Male: Large, familiar black-and-white bird of the lakes. The breeding adult has checkerboard back with white necklace, black head and deep red eyes with long, pointed black bill. Winter has an entirely gray body and bill.

Female: same as male

Juvenile: gray version of adult, without red eyes

Nest: platform, on the ground; female and male build; 1 brood per year

Eggs: 2; olive brown, occasionally brown markings

Incubation: 26-31 days; female and male incubate

Fledging: 75-80 days; female and male feed young

Migration: complete, to southern states, the Gulf coast and Mexico

Food: fish, aquatic insects

Compare: Double-crested Cormorant (pg. 29) has a yellow bill and black chest.

Stan's Notes: A true symbol of the wildness of our lakes. Prefers clear lakes because it hunts for fish by eyesight. Legs are set so far back that it has a hard time walking on land, but it's a great swimmer. Its name comes from the Swedish word *lom*, meaning "lame," for the awkward way it walks on land. Its unique call suggests the wild laughter of a demented person, and led to the phrase "crazy as a loon." Young ride on the backs of swimming parents. Adults will perform distraction displays to protect young. Very sensitive to disturbance during nesting and will abandon nest.

soaring

juvenile

BALD EAGLE
Haliaeetus leucocephalus

YEAR-ROUND
MIGRATION

Size: 31-37" (79-94 cm); up to 7-foot wingspan

Male: Pure white head and tail contrast with dark brown-to-black body and wings. A large, curved yellow bill and yellow feet.

Female: same as male, only slightly larger

Juvenile: dark brown with white spots or speckles throughout body and wings, gray bill

Nest: massive platform; female and male build; 1 brood per year

Eggs: 2; off-white, unmarked

Incubation: 34-36 days; female and male incubate

Fledging: 75-90 days; female and male feed young

Migration: partial migrator, to southeastern states

Food: fish, carrion, ducks

Compare: Larger than the Black Vulture (pg. 23) and Turkey Vulture (pg. 25). Black Vulture has a shorter tail and lacks adult Bald Eagle's white head and tail. Turkey Vulture flies with its two-toned wings held in a V, unlike the straight-out wing position of Eagle.

Stan's Notes: There are more Bald Eagles in Florida than in any other of the contiguous 48 states. Uses same nest year after year, adding sticks, enlarging it to massive proportions, at times up to 1,000 pounds. In the midair mating ritual, one bird flips upside down, locking talons with another. Both tumble until they break apart to continue flying. Thought to mate for life, but will switch mates if not successful reproducing. Juveniles attain white head and tail at about 4 to 5 years of age.

WOOD STORK
Mycteria americana

YEAR-ROUND
SUMMER

Size: 40" (102 cm); up to 5-foot wingspan

Male: An all-white body with a bald, nearly black head and thick, slightly down-curved dark bill. Tail, wing tips and entire trailing edge of wings are black, as seen in flight. Black legs and pink feet.

Female: same as male

Juvenile: similar to adult, but a gray-to-brown head and neck, dull yellow bill

Nest: platform; female and male build; 1 brood per year

Eggs: 2-4; white without markings

Incubation: 28-32 days; male and female incubate

Fledging: 55-60 days; female and male feed young

Migration: complete, to southern coastal states, non-migrator in most of Florida

Food: fish, amphibians, aquatic insects, snails

Compare: Similar size as Great Egret (pg. 317), which lacks Stork's dark head and down-curved bill. Nearly twice the size of Snowy Egret (pg. 311). Look for a black tail and wings.

Stan's Notes: A year-round Florida resident, on state and federal endangered species lists. Like many wading birds, it has less than 20 percent of its population 100 years ago. Feeds by swinging its open bill through water until it contacts prey, then snaps shut. Can be seen shuffling its feet, stirring up fish before capturing. Nests in large colonies, usually high in trees. Usually doesn't breed until age 4 or 5 years. Will abandon eggs or young if food supply is short.

BLUE-GRAY GNATCATCHER
Polioptila caerulea

YEAR-ROUND
WINTER

Size: 4" (10 cm)

Male: Light blue head, back and wings, and white chest. Long black tail with white undertail, often held cocked above rest of the body. Black eyebrows. Prominent white eye ring.

Female: same as male, only grayer

Juvenile: same as adult

Nest: cup; female and male build; 1 brood a year

Eggs: 4-5; pale blue with dark markings

Incubation: 10-13 days; female and male incubate

Fledging: 10-12 days; female and male feed young

Migration: complete, to Florida, other southern states, Bahamas, Central America, non-migrator in most of Florida

Food: insects

Compare: The only small blue bird with a black tail. Constantly flicks its tail up and down and from side to side. Very active near the nest, look for it flitting around upper branches in search of insects.

Stan's Notes: Found throughout Florida in a wide variety of forest types, listen for its wheezy call notes to help locate. A fun and easy bird to watch as it cocks and fans tail while calling. Many northern Blue-gray Gnatcatchers will winter in Florida. In many years, it nests so early that by mid-June it is no longer defending territory. Like many open woodland nesters, it is a common cowbird host. Although the population is abundant and widespread, it has been decreasing in the recent past.

73

TREE SWALLOW
Tachycineta bicolor

YEAR-ROUND
MIGRATION

Size: 5-6" (13-15 cm)

Male: Blue green in the spring and greener in fall. Appears to change color in direct sunlight. A white belly, a notched tail and pointed wing tips.

Female: similar to male, only duller

Juvenile: gray brown with a white belly and grayish breast band

Nest: cavity; female and male line former woodpecker cavity or nest box; 1 brood per year

Eggs: 4-6; white, unmarked

Incubation: 13-16 days; female incubates

Fledging: 20-24 days; female and male feed young

Migration: complete, to Mexico and Central America, winters in most of Florida

Food: insects

Compare: Similar color to Purple Martin (pg. 83), but smaller and has white chest and belly. Barn Swallow (pg. 79) has rust belly and deeply forked tail.

Stan's Notes: A year-round Florida resident. Most common along coastal beaches, freshwater ponds and lakes, agricultural fields. Is attracted to your yard with a nest box. Competes with the Eastern Bluebird for nest boxes. Will travel great distances to find dropped feathers to line its grass nest. Sometimes seen playing, chasing after dropped feathers. Often seen flying back and forth across open fields, feeding on insects. Gathers in large flocks during winter.

female pg. 109

male

INDIGO BUNTING
Passerina cyanea

Size: 5½" (14 cm)

Male: Vibrant blue finch-like bird. Scattered dark markings on wings and tail.

Female: light brown bird with faint markings

Juvenile: similar to female

Nest: cup; female builds; 2 broods per year

Eggs: 3-4; pale blue, unmarked

Incubation: 12-13 days; female incubates

Fledging: 10-11 days; female feeds young

Migration: complete, to southern states, Mexico and Central America

Food: insects, seeds, fruit, will visit seed feeders

Compare: Smaller than Eastern Bluebird (pg. 81) and lacking Bluebird's red chest patch.

Stan's Notes: Usually only the males are noticed. Actually a black bird, as it doesn't have any blue pigment in its feathers. As with Blue Jays, the sunlight is refracted within the structure of the bunting's feathers, making them appear blue. Appears iridescent in direct sunlight. Molts to acquire body feathers with gray tips, which quickly wear off to reveal bright blue plumage. Males often sing from treetops to attract mates. Will come to feeders in spring before insects are plentiful. Mostly seen along woodland edges, feeding on insects. Migrates at night in flocks of five to ten birds. A late migrant, with males returning before the females and juveniles. Males nearly always return to previous year's nest site. Juveniles move to within a mile from birth site.

BARN SWALLOW
Hirundo rustica

MIGRATION
SUMMER

Size: 7" (18 cm)

Male: A sleek swallow with a blue black back, a cinnamon belly and a reddish brown chin. White spots on long forked tail.

Female: same as male, only slightly duller

Juvenile: similar to adult, with tan belly and chin and shorter tail

Nest: cup; female and male build; 2 broods a year

Eggs: 4-5; white with brown markings

Incubation: 13-17 days; female incubates

Fledging: 18-23 days; female and male feed young

Migration: complete, to South America

Food: insects, prefers beetles, wasps and flies

Compare: Tree Swallow (pg. 75) has white belly and chin, and notched tail. The Chimney Swift (pg. 97) has narrow pointed tail with wings longer than the body. The Purple Martin (pg. 83) is nearly 2 inches larger and has a dark purple belly.

Stan's Notes: Of the eight swallow species in Florida, this is the only one with a deeply forked tail. Unlike other swallows, the Barn Swallow rarely glides in flight, so look for continuous flapping. It builds a mud nest using up to 1,000 beak-loads of mud, often in or on barns. Nests in colonies of four to six, but nesting alone is not uncommon. Drinks while flying by skimming water or getting water from wet leaves. It also bathes while flying through the rain or sprinklers.

male

female

EASTERN BLUEBIRD
Sialia sialis

YEAR-ROUND

Size: 7" (18 cm)

Male: Reminiscent of its larger cousin, American Robin, with a rusty red breast and white belly. Sky blue head, back and tail.

Female: shares rusty red breast and white belly, but is grayer with faint blue tail and wings

Juvenile: similar to female, with spots on chest, blue wing markings

Nest: cavity, old woodpecker cavity or man-made nest box; female builds; 2 broods per year

Eggs: 4-5; pale blue, unmarked

Incubation: 12-14 days; female incubates

Fledging: 15-18 days; male and female feed young

Migration: complete, to southern states, winters in most of Florida

Food: insects, fruit

Compare: Male Indigo Bunting (pg. 77) is nearly all blue, lacking rusty red chest. The Blue Jay (pg. 87) is considerably larger with a crest and white markings.

Stan's Notes: Year-round resident that is joined by many northern migrants, swelling populations each winter. Once nearly eliminated from Florida due to a lack of nesting cavities, bluebirds have made a remarkable comeback with the aid of bird enthusiasts who have put up thousands of bluebird boxes. Easily tamed, they will come to a shallow dish with mealworms. Will perch in trees or on fence posts and wait for grasshoppers. Gives a distinctive "chur-lee chur chur-lee" song. Young of first brood help raise young of second.

male

female

PURPLE MARTIN
Progne subis

SUMMER

Size: 8½" (22 cm)

Male: A large swallow-shaped bird with a purple head, back and belly. Black wings and tail. Notched tail.

Female: gray purple head and back with a whitish belly, darker wings and tail

Juvenile: same as female

Nest: cavity; female and male line the cavity of house; 1 brood per year

Eggs: 4-5; white, unmarked

Incubation: 15-18 days; female incubates

Fledging: 26-30 days; male and female feed young

Migration: complete, to South America

Food: insects

Compare: The male is the only dark-purple-bellied swallow. Usually only seen in groups.

Stan's Notes: Largest swallow species in North America. Formerly nested in tree cavities, but now nearly exclusively nests in man-made nest boxes in Florida. Main diet consists of dragonflies, not mosquitoes as once thought. Often drinks and bathes while flying by skimming water or flying through rain. Returns to the same nest site each year. Males arrive before the females and yearlings. Often nests within 100 feet of a human dwelling and, in fact, the most successful colonies are located within this distance. Young strike out to form new colonies. Huge colonies gather in fall to migrate to South America.

YEAR-ROUND

BLUE JAY
Cyanocitta cristata

Size: 12" (30 cm)

Male: Large bright-light-blue and white bird with black necklace. Crest moves up and down at will. White face with a gray belly. White wing bars on blue wings. Black spots and a white tip on blue tail.

Female: same as male

Juvenile: same as adult, only duller

Nest: cup; the female and male build; 1-2 broods per year

Eggs: 4-5; green to blue with brown markings

Incubation: 16-18 days; female incubates

Fledging: 17-21 days; female and male feed young

Migration: non-migrator to partial migrator, will move around to find abundant food source

Food: insects, fruit, carrion, seeds, nuts, attracted to seed feeders

Compare: Slightly larger than the Florida Scrub-Jay (pg. 85), which is darker blue. The Eastern Bluebird (pg. 81) is much smaller and lacks crest. Belted Kingfisher (pg. 89) lacks vivid blue color and black necklace.

Stan's Notes: Highly intelligent bird, solving problems, gathering food and communicating more than other birds. Screams like a hawk to scatter birds at a feeder before approaching. The alarm of the forest, screams at any intruders in woods. Known to eat eggs or young birds from other nests. One of the few birds to cache food. Feathers lack blue pigment; refracted sunlight casts blue light.

male

female

BELTED KINGFISHER
Ceryle alcyon

YEAR-ROUND
WINTER

Size: 13" (33 cm)

Male: Large blue bird with white belly. Broad blue gray breast band and a ragged crest that is raised and lowered at will. Large head with a long, thick black bill. A small white spot directly in front of red brown eyes. Black wing tips with splashes of white that flash when flying.

Female: same as male, but with rusty breast band in addition to blue gray band, and rusty flanks

Juvenile: same as adult

Nest: cavity; female and male excavate; 1 brood per year

Eggs: 6-7; white, unmarked

Incubation: 23-24 days; female and male incubate

Fledging: 23-24 days; female and male feed young

Migration: complete, to southern states, Central and South America, winters in Florida

Food: small fish

Compare: Similar in size to the Blue Jay (pg. 87), but Kingfisher is darker blue with larger, more ragged crest.

Stan's Notes: Seen perched on branches near the water, it dives headfirst for small fish and returns to a branch to eat. Has a loud machine-gun-like call. Excavates a deep cavity in bank of river or lake. Parents drop dead fish into water, teaching young to dive. Regurgitates pellets of bone after meals, being unable to pass bones through digestive tract. Mates recognize each other by call.

89

PURPLE GALLINULE
Porphyrula martinica

YEAR-ROUND
SUMMER

Size: 13" (33 cm)

Male: A vibrant blue head, chest and belly with iridescent green back and wings. A yellow-tipped red bill. White undertail. Yellow legs.

Female: same as male

Juvenile: brown version of adult, bronze legs

Nest: ground; female and male build; 1-2 broods per year

Eggs: 6-8; brown with dark markings

Incubation: 22-25 days; female and male incubate

Fledging: 55-60 days; female and male feed young

Migration: complete, to West Indies, Central America, South America, winters in southern Florida

Food: insects, snails, seeds, berries, frogs

Compare: Similar size as the American Coot (pg. 15), which lacks the Gallinule's yellow-tipped red bill. Similar size as Common Moorhen (pg. 13), but is differentiated by the lack of Moorhen's white side stripe. Look for the white undertail feathers to help identify.

Stan's Notes: One of Florida's most dramatic-looking birds, it is commonly seen in the Everglades. Uses its extremely long toes to walk on floating vegetation in freshwater and saltwater marshes, hunting for grasshoppers and other insects, grains and frogs. Family groups stay together, with the first brood sometimes helping to raise the second. Can be seen year-round in the southern part of the state, but moves out of northern Florida during winter. Known for individuals to wander well north of the state.

non-breeding adult

white juvenile

breeding

molting juvenile

LITTLE BLUE HERON
Egretta caerulea

YEAR-ROUND
SUMMER

Size: 24" (60 cm)

Male: Dark slate blue to purple nearly all year. Dull green legs, feet. Black-tipped blue-gray bill. Breeding has several long plumes on crown with reddish-purple head and neck.

Female: same as male

Juvenile: pure white overall, yellowish legs and feet, black-tipped gray bill

Nest: platform; female and male build; 1 brood per year

Eggs: 2-6; light blue without markings

Incubation: 20-23 days; female and male incubate

Fledging: 42-49 days; female and male feed young

Migration: complete, to Central and South America, winters in most of Florida

Food: fish, aquatic insects

Compare: Breeding adult lacks Tricolored's (pg. 95) white belly. Juvenile is confused with the Snowy Egret (pg. 311), which has bright yellow feet, black legs and solid black bill. Breeding Cattle Egret (pg. 309) has orange buff crest, breast and back, red-orange bill.

Stan's Notes: Unusual because young look completely different from adults. All-white young turn blotchy white the first year. By second year they look like adult birds. A very slow stalker of prey, feeding in freshwater lakes and rivers, saltwater marshes and wetlands. Nests in large colonies near saltwater sites. Often flies north after breeding season, returning to Florida for the winter.

TRICOLORED HERON
Egretta tricolor

YEAR-ROUND
SUMMER

Size: 26" (66 cm)

Male: Dark blue head, neck and wings contrast with a white belly and neck. Small brown patches at base of neck with lighter brown on lower back. A long, slender yellow bill with a dark tip. Yellow-to-pale-green legs.

Female: same as male

Juvenile: similar to adult, chestnut brown in place of dark blue areas

Nest: platform; female and male build; 1 brood per year

Eggs: 3-6; light blue without markings

Incubation: 21-25 days; female and male incubate

Fledging: 32-35 days; female and male feed young

Migration: complete, to Central America, winters in most of Florida

Food: fish, aquatic insects

Compare: Great Blue Heron (pg. 265) is much larger and lacks white undersides. The Little Blue Heron (pg. 93) is slightly smaller and lacks the Tricolored's yellow bill and white belly.

Stan's Notes: A medium-sized heron characterized by its white undersides. Like other herons, the Tricolored has declined in numbers due to wetland habitat loss. To hunt, it stands still and waits. Will also chase after small fish. Mainly in saltwater marshes and estuaries, but also in freshwater marshes inland. Known to wander as far as Kansas. Colony nester with other herons, one adult always on duty at the nest. Was not hunted for plumes like other herons.

CHIMNEY SWIFT
Chaetura pelagica

SUMMER

Size: 5" (13 cm)

Male: Nondescript, swallow-shaped bird, usually only seen flying. Long, thin all-brown body with a pointed tail and head. Long swept-back wings are longer than body.

Female: same as male

Juvenile: same as adult

Nest: half cup; female and male build; 1 brood per year

Eggs: 4-5; white, unmarked

Incubation: 19-21 days; female and male incubate

Fledging: 28-30 days; female and male feed young

Migration: complete, to South America

Food: insects, while in flight

Compare: Considerably smaller than Purple Martin (pg. 83) and lacks Martin's iridescent purple color. Barn Swallow (pg. 79) has forked tail, compared with the pointed tail of the Chimney Swift. Tree Swallow (pg. 75) has white belly and blue green back.

Stan's Notes: One of the fastest flyers in the bird world. Spends all day flying, rarely perching. Bathes and drinks by skimming across water surfaces. Unique in-flight twittering call is often heard before bird is seen. Flies in groups, feeding on flying insects nearly 100 feet in the air. Often called the Flying Cigar due to its pointed body shape. Hundreds will nest and roost in large chimneys, hence the common name. Nest, made of tiny twigs, is cemented with saliva and attached to inside of chimney or hollow tree.

YEAR-ROUND
WINTER

CHIPPING SPARROW
Spizella passerina

Size: 5" (13 cm)

Male: Small gray brown sparrow with a clear gray chest, rusty crown, white eyebrows with a black eye line, thin gray black bill and two faint wing bars.

Female: same as male

Juvenile: similar to adult, but has streaked chest and lacks rusty cap

Nest: cup; female builds; 2 broods per year

Eggs: 3-5; blue green with brown markings

Incubation: 11-14 days; female incubates

Fledging: 10-12 days; female and male feed young

Migration: complete, to southern states, Mexico and Central America, winters in Florida

Food: insects, seeds, will come to ground feeders

Compare: Smaller than the Song Sparrow (pg. 105), which has a heavily streaked chest. Female House Finch (pg. 101) also has a streaked chest, compared with the unmarked chest of Chipping Sparrow.

Stan's Notes: A winter resident in Florida, seen from October to May. Common garden or yard bird, often seen feeding on dropped seeds below feeders. Gathers in large family groups to feed each spring in preparation for migration. Migrates at night in flocks of 20 to 30 birds. Received its common name from the male's slow "chip" call. Often just called Chippy. Nest is placed low in dense shrubs and is almost always lined with animal hair. Doesn't nest in the state.

male pg. 289

female

HOUSE FINCH
Carpodacus mexicanus

YEAR-ROUND

Size: 5" (13 cm)

Female: A plain brown bird with a heavily streaked white chest.

Male: orange red face, chest and rump, a brown cap, brown marking behind eyes, brown wings streaked with white, white belly with brown streaks

Juvenile: similar to female

Nest: cup, sometimes in cavities; female builds; 2 broods per year

Eggs: 4-5; pale blue, lightly marked

Incubation: 12-14 days; female incubates

Fledging: 15-19 days; female and male feed young

Migration: non-migrator to partial migrator, will move around to find food

Food: seeds, fruit, leaf buds, will visit seed feeders

Compare: The female Purple Finch (pg. 111) is very similar, but the female House Finch lacks the bold white eyebrows. Female American Goldfinch (pg. 323) has a clear chest and white wing bars.

Stan's Notes: The House Finch was originally introduced to Long Island, New York, in the 1940s from western America. A very social bird, it visits feeders in small flocks. Seems to prefer nesting in hanging flower baskets. Incubating female is fed by male. Loud and cheerful warbling song. Suffers from a fatal eye disease that causes the eyes to crust over.

HOUSE WREN
Troglodytes aedon

WINTER

Size: 5" (13 cm)

Male: A small all-brown bird with lighter brown marking on tail and wings. Brown, slightly curved bill. Often holds its tail erect.

Female: same as male

Juvenile: same as adult

Nest: cavity; female and male line just about any cavity; 2 broods per year

Eggs: 4-6; tan with brown markings

Incubation: 10-13 days; female and male incubate

Fledging: 12-15 days; female and male feed young

Migration: complete, to southern states and Mexico

Food: insects

Compare: House Wren is distinguished from Carolina Wren (pg. 107) by the lack of eye stripe.

Stan's Notes: A prolific songster, it will sing from dawn until dusk during the mating season. Easily attracted to nest boxes. In spring, the male chooses several prospective nesting cavities and places a few small twigs in each. Female inspects each, chooses one, and finishes the nest building. She will completely fill the nest cavity with uniformly small twigs, then line a small depression at back of cavity with pine needles and grass. Often has trouble fitting long twigs through nest cavity hole. Tries many different directions and approaches until successful.

WINTER

SONG SPARROW
Melospiza melodia

Size: 5-6" (13-15 cm)

Male: Common brown sparrow with heavy dark streaks on chest coalescing into a central dark spot.

Female: same as male

Juvenile: similar to adult, finely streaked chest without central spot

Nest: cup; female builds; 2 broods per year

Eggs: 3-4; pale blue to green with reddish brown markings

Incubation: 12-14 days; female incubates

Fledging: 9-12 days; female and male feed young

Migration: complete, to southern states

Food: insects, seeds, rarely visits seed feeders

Compare: Similar to other brown sparrows, look for a heavily streaked chest with central dark spot.

Stan's Notes: Many Song Sparrow subspecies or varieties, but dark central spot carries through each variant. While the female builds another nest for second brood, the male often takes over feeding the young. Returns to similar area each year, defending a small territory by singing from thick shrubs. Common host of the Brown-headed Cowbird. Ground feeders, look for them to scratch simultaneously with both feet to expose seeds. Unlike many sparrow species, Song Sparrows rarely flock together.

CAROLINA WREN
Thryothorus ludovicianus

YEAR-ROUND

Size: 5½" (14 cm)

Male: Warm rusty-brown head and back with an orange yellow chest and belly. White throat and a prominent white eye stripe. A short stubby tail, often cocked up.

Female: same as male

Juvenile: same as adult

Nest: cavity; female and male build; 2 broods per year, sometimes 3

Eggs: 4-6; white, sometimes pink or creamy, with brown markings

Incubation: 12-14 days; female incubates

Fledging: 12-14 days; female and male feed young

Migration: non-migrator

Food: insects, fruit, few seeds

Compare: Similar to the House Wren (pg. 103), but the Carolina Wren is lighter brown and has a prominent white eye stripe.

Stan's Notes: Mates are long-term, remaining together throughout the year in permanent territories. Will sing throughout the year. The male is known to sing up to 40 different song types, singing one song repeatedly before switching to another. Females also sing, resulting in duets. Male often takes over feeding the first brood of young while the female renests. Will nest in birdhouses or in the most unusual places, such as mailboxes, bumpers of cars, broken taillights or just about any other cavity. Found in woodland or brushy yards.

107

female

male pg. 77

INDIGO BUNTING
Passerina cyanea

MIGRATION
SUMMER
WINTER

Size: 5½" (14 cm)

Female: Light brown finch-like bird. Faint streaking on a light tan chest. Wings have a very faint blue cast with indistinct wing bars.

Male: vibrant blue finch-like bird, scattered dark markings on wings and tail

Juvenile: similar to female

Nest: cup; female builds; 2 broods per year

Eggs: 3-4; pale blue, unmarked

Incubation: 12-13 days; female incubates

Fledging: 10-11 days; female feeds young

Migration: complete, to southern states, Mexico and Central America

Food: insects, seeds, fruit, will visit seed feeders

Compare: Similar to female finches. Female American Goldfinch (pg. 323) has white wing bars. Female Purple Finch (pg. 111) has white eyebrows and a heavily streaked chest. The female House Finch (pg. 101) also has a heavily streaked chest.

Stan's Notes: A secretive bird, usually only the males are seen. Males often sing from treetops to attract mates. Will come to feeders in spring before insects are plentiful. Mostly seen along woodland edges, feeding on insects. Migrates at night in flocks of five to ten birds. A late migrant, with males returning before the females and juveniles. Juveniles move to within a mile from birth site.

male pg. 291

female

PURPLE FINCH
Carpodacus purpureus

WINTER

Size: 6" (15 cm)

Female: A plain brown bird with a heavily streaked chest. Prominent white eyebrows.

Male: raspberry-red head, cap, breast, back and rump, brownish wings and tail

Juvenile: same as female

Nest: cup; female and male build; 1 brood a year

Eggs: 4-5; greenish blue with brown markings

Incubation: 12-13 days; female incubates

Fledging: 13-14 days; female and male feed young

Migration: irruptive, moves around in search of food

Food: seeds, insects, fruit, comes to seed feeders

Compare: Female House Finch (pg. 101) lacks female Purple Finch's white eyebrows. The female American Goldfinch (pg. 323) has a clear chest and white wing bars.

Stan's Notes: Usually only seen during winter in northern Florida, when flocks of Purple Finches leave their homes farther north and move around looking for food. Travels in flocks of up to 50. Comes to seed feeders along with House Finches, making it hard to tell them apart. A rich loud song and a distinctive "tic" note is made only in flight. Not a purple color, the Latin name *purpureus* means "crimson" or other reddish color.

111

YEAR-ROUND

HOUSE SPARROW
Passer domesticus

Size: 6" (15 cm)

Male: Medium sparrow-like bird with large black spot on throat extending down to the chest. Brown back and single white wing bars. A gray belly and crown.

Female: all-light-brown bird, slightly smaller, lacks the black throat patch and single wing bars

Juvenile: similar to female

Nest: domed cup nest, within cavity; female and male build; 2-3 broods per year

Eggs: 4-6; white with brown markings

Incubation: 10-12 days; female incubates

Fledging: 14-17 days; female and male feed young

Migration: non-migrator, moves around to find food

Food: seeds, insects, fruit, comes to seed feeders

Compare: Lacks the rusty crown of Chipping Sparrow (pg. 99). Look for male House Sparrow's black bib. Female has a clear chest and no marking on head (cap).

Stan's Notes: Introduced from Europe to Central Park, New York, in 1850 and now found throughout North America. These birds are not really sparrows, but members of the Weaver Finch family, characterized by large, oversized domed nests. Constructs a nest containing scraps of plastic, paper and whatever else is available. Aggressive bird that will kill the young of other birds in order to take over a cavity. Familiar city bird, nearly always in flocks.

winter pg. 215

breeding

LEAST SANDPIPER
Calidris minutilla

Size: 6" (15 cm)

Male: Dull yellow legs. Short, down-curved black bill. White belly. Breeding adult has golden brown head and back, and white eyebrows.

Female: same as male

Juvenile: similar to winter adult, but buff brown and lacking the breast band

Nest: ground; the male and female build; 1 brood per year

Eggs: 3-4; olive with dark markings

Incubation: 19-23 days; male and female incubate

Fledging: 25-28 days; male and female feed young

Migration: complete, to southern coastal states and Central America

Food: insects, aquatic insects, seeds

Compare: The smallest of sandpipers. Often confused with breeding Western Sandpiper (pg. 117) and Semipalmated Sandpiper (pg. 217), Least Sandpiper's yellow legs differentiate it from other tiny sandpipers. The short, thin, down-curved bill also helps to identify.

Stan's Notes: Winters all along the southern coastal states from Florida to California. It's the smallest of the peeps (sandpipers) that nest on the tundra in northern parts of Canada and Alaska. The yellow legs can be difficult to see in water, poor light or if covered with mud. Prefers the grassy flats of both saltwater and freshwater ponds. A tame sandpiper that can be approached without scaring.

winter pg. 219

breeding

WESTERN SANDPIPER
Calidris mauri

MIGRATION
WINTER

Size: 6½" (16 cm)

Male: Black legs. Narrow bill that droops near tip. Breeding has bright rusty-brown crown, ear patch and back with white chin and chest.

Female: same as male

Juvenile: similar to breeding adult, bright buff brown on back only

Nest: ground; the male and female build; 1 brood per year

Eggs: 2-4; light brown with dark markings

Incubation: 20-22 days; male and female incubate

Fledging: 19-21 days; male and female feed young

Migration: complete, to southern coastal states and Central America

Food: insects, aquatic insects

Compare: Is often confused with the breeding Least Sandpiper (pg. 115) and the Semipalmated Sandpiper (pg. 217), but bright rust-brown crown, ear patch and back help to identify. Look for black legs to differentiate from the Least Sandpiper. Western has a longer bill that droops slightly at tip.

Stan's Notes: A winter resident of Florida, it also winters all along the southern coastal states from Florida to California. Nests on the ground in large "loose" colonies on the tundra of northern coastal Alaska. Adults leave breeding grounds several weeks before the young. Some will obtain breeding plumage before leaving Florida in spring. Feeds in deeper water than the Semipalmated Sandpiper.

117

SEMIPALMATED PLOVER
Charadrius semipalmatus

Size: 7" (18 cm)

Male: A brown-backed bird with black necklace and short, black-tipped orange bill. White patch on forehead. White chest and belly. Breeding has black mask, orange eye ring.

Female: same as male

Juvenile: similar to adult, lacking well-defined black necklace

Nest: ground; male builds; 1 brood per year

Eggs: 3-4; light brown with dark markings

Incubation: 23-25 days; male and female incubate

Fledging: 22-28 days; male and female feed young

Migration: complete, to southern coastal states, and Central and South America

Food: insects, seeds, worms

Compare: Smaller than Killdeer (pg. 149) and with only one black necklace, compared with the two of Killdeer. Look for a solid dark back with a very short bill to help identify the Semipalmated Plover.

Stan's Notes: A winter resident of Florida, it also winters all along the southern coastal states from Florida to California. Nests on the ground on the tundra of northern Canada and Alaska. Prefers to nest in open rocky places, where the male scrapes out a shallow depression. Breeding birds often have orange eye rings. Often seen in mixed flocks with Semipalmated Sandpipers. Hunts by running quickly, stopping to look, then stabbing prey. Population decreased dramatically during the late 1800s due to hunting.

male pg. 3

female

EASTERN TOWHEE
Pipilo erythrophthalmus

Size: 7-8" (18-20 cm)

Female: A mostly light brown bird. Rusty red brown sides and white belly. Long brown tail with white tip. Short, stout, pointed bill. White wing patches flash in flight. Off-white eyes.

Male: similar to female, but is black, not brown

Juvenile: light brown, a heavily streaked head, chest and belly, long dark tail with white tip

Nest: cup; female builds; 2 broods per year

Eggs: 3-4; creamy white with brown markings

Incubation: 12-13 days; female incubates

Fledging: 10-12 days; female and male feed young

Migration: complete, to southern states and South America, winters in Florida

Food: insects, seeds, fruit, visits ground feeders

Compare: Slightly smaller than the American Robin (pg. 239).

Stan's Notes: Common name comes from its distinctive "tow-hee" call given by both sexes. Mostly known for its characteristic call that sounds like, "Drink-your-tea!" Seen hopping backward with both feet to rake up leaf litter (bilateral scratching), in search of insects and seeds. The female broods, but male does most of the feeding of young. White-eyed form in Florida.

CEDAR WAXWING
Bombycilla cedrorum

WINTER

Size: 7½" (19 cm)

Male: Very sleek-looking gray-to-brown bird with pointed crest, light yellow belly and bandit-like black mask. Tip of tail is bright yellow and the tips of wings look as if they have been dipped in red wax.

Female: same as male

Juvenile: slightly smaller, lacking the red wing tips, black mask and sleek appearance, has a heavily streaked chest

Nest: cup; female and male build; 1 brood a year, occasionally 2

Eggs: 4-6; pale blue with brown markings

Incubation: 10-12 days; female incubates

Fledging: 14-18 days; female and male feed young

Migration: partial migrator

Food: cedar cones, fruit, insects

Compare: Nearly identical to its larger, less common cousin, the Bohemian Waxwing.

Stan's Notes: The name is derived from its red wax-like wing tips and preference for eating small blueberry-like cones of the cedar. Wanders in winter to find available food supplies. Mostly seen in flocks, moving from area to area, looking for berries. Spends most of its time at the tops of tall trees. Listen for the very high-pitched whistling sounds that it constantly makes. In the summer, before berries are abundant, it feeds on insects.

male pg. 5

female

YEAR-ROUND

BROWN-HEADED COWBIRD
Molothrus ater

Size: 7½" (19 cm)

Female: Dull brown bird with no obvious markings. Long, pointed, sharp gray bill.

Male: glossy black bird, chocolate brown head

Juvenile: similar to female, only dull gray color and a streaked chest

Nest: no nest; lays eggs in nests of other birds

Eggs: 5-7; white with brown markings

Incubation: 10-13 days; host bird incubates eggs

Fledging: 10-11 days; host birds feed young

Migration: complete, to southern states, winters in Florida

Food: insects, seeds, will come to seed feeders

Compare: In the blackbird family. The slightly larger female Red-winged Blackbird (pg. 135) has white eyebrows and a streaked chest. The European Starling (pg. 7) has speckles, a long, pointed yellow bill and short tail.

Stan's Notes: Of about 750 species of parasitic birds worldwide, this is the only parasitic bird in Florida, laying all eggs in host birds' nests, leaving others to raise its young. Cowbirds are known to have laid eggs in nests of over 200 species of birds. Some birds reject cowbird eggs, but most raise them, even to the exclusion of their own young. Look for warblers and other birds feeding young birds twice their own size. At one time cowbirds followed bison to feed on the insects attracted to the animals.

breeding

winter

SPOTTED SANDPIPER
Actitis macularia

MIGRATION
WINTER

Size: 8" (20 cm)

Male: Long dull yellow legs and a long bill. Olive brown back. White chest and a white line over eyes. Winter adult lacks breast spots. Breeding adult has black spots on chest.

Female: same as male

Juvenile: similar to winter adult, with a darker bill

Nest: ground; female and male build; 2 broods per year

Eggs: 3-4; brownish with brown markings

Incubation: 20-24 days; male incubates

Fledging: 17-21 days; male feeds young

Migration: complete, to southern states and South America

Food: aquatic insects

Compare: Much smaller than the Greater Yellowlegs (pg. 161) and Lesser Yellowlegs (pg. 143). Look for Spotted Sandpiper to bob its tail up and down while standing. Look for the breeding Spotted Sandpiper's black spots extending from chest down to abdomen.

Stan's Notes: One of the more common sandpipers. Constantly bobs its tail while standing and walks as if delicately balanced. Flies with wings held in a cup-like arc, rarely lifting them above a horizontal plane. Is able to fly straight up out of water. One of the few shorebirds that actually dives underwater if pursued. Female mates with multiple males and lays eggs in up to five different nests. Male incubates and cares for young. In winter plumage, it lacks spots.

winter pg. 229

breeding

SANDERLING
Calidris canutus

Size: 8" (20 cm)

Male: Black legs and bill. During breeding season (April to August) the head, chest and back are rusty colored, and belly is white.

Female: same as male

Juvenile: spotty black on head and back, with white belly, black legs and bill

Nest: ground; male builds; 1-2 broods per year

Eggs: 3-4; greenish-olive with brown markings

Incubation: 24-30 days; male and female incubate

Fledging: 16-17 days; female and male feed young

Migration: partial migrator to complete, to West Indies and East, Gulf and South American coasts

Food: insects

Compare: Same size as the breeding plumage Spotted Sandpiper (pg. 127), but lacks chest spots.

Stan's Notes: One of the most common shorebirds in the state, but mostly seen in gray winter plumage from August to April. Can be seen in groups on sandy beaches, running out with each retreating wave to feed. Look for a flash of white on wings when in flight. Occasionally the female will mate with several males (polyandry), resulting in males and the female incubating separate nests. Both sexes will perform a distraction display if threatened. Nests in the Arctic tundra. Declining in populations. Surveys show a greater than 80 percent decline in numbers since the 1970s.

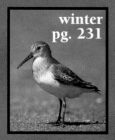

winter
pg. 231

breeding

DUNLIN
Calidris alpina

WINTER

Size: 8-9" (20-22.5 cm)

Male: Black legs. Stout bill curved slightly down-ward at the tip. Distinctive breeding adult has a rusty red back, a finely streaked chest and an obvious black patch on the belly.

Female: slightly larger than male, with longer bill

Juvenile: slightly rusty back with spotty chest

Nest: ground; the male and female build; 1 brood per year

Eggs: 2-4; an olive-buff or a blue-green with red-brown markings

Incubation: 21-22 days; male and female incubate, the male during day, female at night

Fledging: 19-21 days; male feeds young, female often leaves before young fledge

Migration: complete, to southern coastal states and the Central American coast, winters in coastal Florida

Food: insects

Compare: Similar in size to the breeding Sanderling (pg. 129), look for the obvious black belly patch and curved bill of breeding Dunlin.

Stan's Notes: Breeding plumage more common in spring. Flights include heights of 100 feet with brief gliding alternating with shallow flutters, and rhythmic, repeating song. In flight, look for dark center on rump. Huge flocks fly synchronously, with birds twisting and turning, flashing their light and dark undersides. Males tend to fly farther south than females in winter. Doesn't nest in Florida.

male pg. 295

female

NORTHERN CARDINAL
Cardinalis cardinalis

Size: 8-9" (20-22.5 cm)

Female: Buff brown bird with tinges of red on crest and wings, a black mask and large red bill.

Male: red bird with a black mask extending from face down to chin and throat, large red bill and crest

Juvenile: same as female, with blackish gray bill

Nest: cup; female builds; 2-3 broods per year

Eggs: 3-4; bluish white with brown markings

Incubation: 12-13 days; female and male incubate

Fledging: 9-10 days; female and male feed young

Migration: non-migrator

Food: seeds, insects, fruit, comes to seed feeders

Compare: Female Northern Cardinal appears similar to the juvenile male. Look for the female's bright red bill.

Stan's Notes: A familiar backyard bird. Look for the male feeding female during courtship. Male feeds young of the first brood by himself while female builds second nest. The name comes from the Latin word *cardinalis*, which means "important." Very territorial in spring, it will fight its own reflection in a window. Non-territorial during winter, gathering in small flocks of up to 20 birds. Both the male and female sing, and can be heard anytime of year. Listen for its "whata-cheer-cheer-cheer" territorial call in spring.

female

male pg. 9

RED-WINGED BLACKBIRD
Agelaius phoeniceus

YEAR-ROUND

Size: 8½" (22 cm)

Female: Heavily streaked brown bird with a pointed brown bill and white eyebrows.

Male: jet black bird with red and yellow patches on upper wings, pointed black bill

Juvenile: same as female

Nest: cup; female builds; 2-3 broods per year

Eggs: 3-4; bluish green with brown markings

Incubation: 10-12 days; female incubates

Fledging: 11-14 days; female and male feed young

Migration: complete, to southern states, Mexico and Central America, winters in Florida

Food: seeds, insects, will come to seed feeders

Compare: Slightly larger than female Brown-headed Cowbird (pg. 125), which lacks the white eyebrows and streaks on chest.

Stan's Notes: One of the most widespread and numerous birds in Florida. Each fall and winter, migrant and resident Red-wingeds gather in huge numbers (thousands) with other blackbirds to feed in agricultural fields, marshes and wetlands. Male defends territory by singing from the tops of surrounding vegetation. Repeats call from top of cattail while showing off its red and yellow wing bars (epaulets). The nest is usually over shallow water in a thick stand of cattails. Feeds mostly on seeds in spring and fall, switching to insects during summer. Female chooses mate.

in flight

SUMMER

COMMON NIGHTHAWK
Chordeiles minor

Size: 9" (22.5 cm)

Male: A camouflaged brown and white bird with white chin. A distinctive white band across wings and the tail, seen only in flight.

Female: similar to male, but with tan chin, lacks the white tail band

Juvenile: same as adult

Nest: no nest; lays eggs on the ground, usually on rocks, or on rooftop

Eggs: 2; cream with lavender markings

Incubation: 19-20 days; female and male incubate

Fledging: 20-21 days; female and male feed young

Migration: complete, to South America

Food: insects caught in air

Compare: Much larger than Chimney Swift (pg. 97) and smaller than the Chuck-will's-widow (pg. 157), which lacks the white chin and wing band. Look for obvious white wing band of Common Nighthawk in flight.

Stan's Notes: Usually only seen flying at dusk or after sunset, but not uncommon during day. Very noisy bird, repeating a "peenting" call during flight. Alternates slow wing beats with bursts of quick wing beats. Prolific insect eater. Prefers gravel rooftops for nesting. Male's distinctive springtime mating ritual is a steep diving flight terminated with a loud popping noise. One of the first birds to migrate each autumn. Can be more common in cities than in the country. Not as common as the Chuck-will's-widow.

BURROWING OWL
Athene cunicularia

YEAR-ROUND

Size: 9½" (24 cm)

Male: A brown owl with bold white spots, white belly and very long legs. Yellow eyes.

Female: same as male

Juvenile: same as adult, but belly is brown

Nest: cavity, former mammal den, underground; 1 brood per year

Eggs: 6-11; white without markings

Incubation: 21-28 days; female incubates

Fledging: 25-28 days; female and male feed young

Migration: complete, to Central America, winters in southern Florida

Food: insects, mammals, lizards, birds

Compare: Barred Owl (pg. 189) is twice the size of the Burrowing Owl and has dark brown eyes, compared with the Burrowing Owl's yellow eyes. The Eastern Screech-Owl (pg. 237) is slightly smaller and has ear tufts.

Stan's Notes: An owl of fields, open backyards, golf courses and airports. Nests in small family units or in small colonies. Takes over the underground dens of mammals, occasionally widening its den by kicking dirt backward. Lines den with cow pies, horse dung, grass and feathers. Some people have had success attracting these owls to their backyards by creating artificial dens. Often seen in the day, standing and sleeping around the den entrance. Male brings food to incubating female, often moving family to a new den when young are just a few weeks old.

YEAR-ROUND

NORTHERN BOBWHITE
Colinus virginianus

Size: 10" (25 cm)

Male: Short, stocky, mostly brown bird with short gray tail. A prominent white eye stripe and white chin. Reddish brown sides and belly, often with black lines and dots.

Female: similar to male, but with a buff brown eye stripe and chin

Juvenile: smaller and duller than adult

Nest: ground; the female and male build; 1 brood per year

Eggs: 12-15; white to creamy, unmarked

Incubation: 23-24 days; female and male incubate

Fledging: 6-7 days; female and male feed young

Migration: non-migrator

Food: insects, seeds, fruit, will come to ground feeders offering corn and millet

Compare: Mourning Dove (pg. 155) is a light brown, has long pointed tail and lacks white chin.

Stan's Notes: Found throughout the state, but is most common in northern Florida. Moves around in small flocks of 20 birds (often family members), called a covey. The covey often rests together at night, in a tight circle with tails together and heads facing outward, to watch for predators. Males and females perform a distraction display if nests or young are threatened. Nest is a depression in the ground lined with grass. Often pulls nearby vegetation over nest to help conceal it. Prefers shrubs, orchards, hedgerows and pastures. Male gives a rising whistle, "bob-white," heard mainly in spring and summer. Also gives a single "hoy" call year-round.

LESSER YELLOWLEGS
Tringa flavipes

Size: 10-11" (25-28 cm)

Male: Typical sandpiper-type bird with a brown back and wings, and lightly streaked white breast and belly. A thin, straight black bill and long yellow legs.

Female: same as male

Juvenile: same as adult

Nest: ground; female builds; 1 brood per year

Eggs: 3-4; yellowish with brown markings

Incubation: 22-23 days; male and female incubate

Fledging: 18-20 days; male and female lead young to food

Migration: complete, to Florida and South America

Food: aquatic insects, tiny fish

Compare: Nearly a carbon copy of Greater Yellowlegs (pg. 161), only smaller with shorter bill.

Stan's Notes: Usually seen in large flocks, it combs shorelines and mud flats looking for aquatic insects. Most often seen in the head down, tail up position, walking along, looking to snatch up food. Uses its long straight bill to pluck insects and tiny fish from water. Very shy bird that quite often moves into the water prior to taking flight. Has a variety of "flight" notes that it gives when taking off. A member of the group of sandpipers called Tattlers, all of which scream alarm calls when taking flight. Migrates later than Greater Yellowlegs in spring and earlier in fall. Nests on marshes in spruce forests of central Alaska and central Canada. The nest is a simple depression atop a mound of earth.

winter pg. 245

breeding

YEAR-ROUND

SHORT-BILLED DOWITCHER
Limnodromus griseus

Size: 11" (28 cm)

Male: Long, straight black bill. Off-white eyebrow stripe. Dull-yellow-to-green legs and feet. Breeding plumage is an overall rusty brown with heavy black spots throughout. A small amount of white very low on the belly.

Female: same as male

Juvenile: similar to winter adult

Nest: ground; the female and male build; 1 brood per year

Eggs: 3-4; olive green with dark markings

Incubation: 20-21 days; male and female incubate

Fledging: 25-27 days; male and female feed young

Migration: complete, to the southern coastal states and Central America, winters in coastal Florida

Food: insects, snails, worms, leeches, seeds

Compare: Marbled Godwit (pg. 177) is larger and has a two-toned, upturned bill and gray legs. Smaller than the breeding Willet (pg. 165), which has shorter bill, and bold black and white wing linings, as seen in flight.

Stan's Notes: A common year-round resident found along both Florida coasts and inland on freshwater lakes and marshes. With a rapid probing action like a sewing machine, uses its long straight bill to probe deep into sand and mud for insects. Can be seen with the less common Long-billed Dowitcher (not shown), but it's hard to tell the two apart.

YEAR-ROUND

BROWN THRASHER
Toxostoma rufum

Size: 11" (28 cm)

Male: A rusty red bird with long tail and heavily streaked chest and belly. Two white wing bars. Long curved bill. Bright yellow eyes.

Female: same as male

Juvenile: same as adult, eye color is grayish

Nest: cup; female and male build; 2 broods a year

Eggs: 4-5; pale blue with brown markings

Incubation: 11-14 days; female and male incubate

Fledging: 10-13 days; female and male feed young

Migration: complete, to southern states, winters in Florida

Food: insects, fruit

Compare: Slightly larger in size and similar in shape to the American Robin (pg. 239) and Gray Catbird (pg. 233), but the Thrasher has a streaked chest and rusty color.

Stan's Notes: Year-round resident throughout Florida, with populations swelling during winter months from the influx of northern birds. A prodigious songster, often found in thick shrubs where it sings deliberate musical phrases, repeating each twice. The male has the largest documented song repertoire of all North American birds, with over 1,100 song types. Is often seen quickly flying or running in and out of thick or dense shrubs.

KILLDEER
Charadrius vociferus

YEAR-ROUND

Size: 11" (28 cm)

Male: An upland shorebird with two black bands around the neck like a necklace. A brown back and white belly. Bright reddish-orange rump, visible in flight.

Female: same as male

Juvenile: similar to adult, but only one neck band

Nest: ground; male builds; 2 broods per year

Eggs: 3-5; tan with brown markings

Incubation: 24-28 days; male and female incubate

Fledging: 25 days; male and female lead their young to food

Migration: complete, to southern states, Mexico and Central America, non-migrator in Florida

Food: insects

Compare: Semipalmated Plover (pg. 119) is smaller, shares the brown back and white belly, but has only one black necklace. Killdeer is the only shorebird with two black neck bands.

Stan's Notes: This bird is known for its broken wing impression, which draws intruders away from nest. Once clear of the nest, the Killdeer takes flight. Nests are only a slight depression in a gravel area, often very difficult to see. Young look like yellow cotton balls on stilts. Able to follow parents and peck for insects soon after birth. Is technically classified as a shorebird, but doesn't live at the shore. Often found in vacant fields or along railroads. Has a very distinctive "kill-jer" call.

male

female

YEAR-ROUND
WINTER

AMERICAN KESTREL
Falco sparverius

Size: 10-12" (25-30 cm)

Male: Rusty brown back and tail. A white chest with dark spots. Double black vertical lines on white face. Blue gray wings. Distinctive wide black band with a white edge on tip of rusty tail.

Female: similar to male, slightly larger, but has rusty brown wings and dark bands on tail

Juvenile: same as adult

Nest: cavity; doesn't build a nest within; 1 brood per year

Eggs: 4-5; white with brown markings

Incubation: 29-31 days; male and female incubate

Fledging: 30-31 days; female and male feed young

Migration: complete, to southern states and Central America, non-migrator in most of Florida

Food: insects, small mammals and birds, reptiles

Compare: Similar to other falcons. Look for the two vertical black stripes on face of Kestrel. No other small bird of prey has rusty-colored back or tail.

Stan's Notes: Formerly called Sparrow Hawk due to its small size. Could be called Grasshopper Hawk because it eats many grasshoppers. Hovers near roads before diving for prey. Adapts quickly to a wooden nest box. Has pointed swept-back wings, seen in flight. Perches nearly upright. Kestrels are rare raptors in that males and females have quite different markings. Watch for them to pump their tails up and down after landing on perches.

female

male

NORTHERN FLICKER
Colaptes auratus

YEAR-ROUND

Size: 12" (30 cm)

Male: Brown and black woodpecker with a large white rump patch visible only when flying. Black necklace above a speckled breast. Red spot on nape of neck and black mustache.

Female: same as male, lacking black mustache

Juvenile: same as adult

Nest: cavity; female and male excavate; 1 brood per year

Eggs: 5-8; white, unmarked

Incubation: 11-14 days; female and male incubate

Fledging: 25-28 days; female and male feed young

Migration: complete, to southern states, non-migrator in Florida

Food: insects, especially ants and beetles

Compare: Yellow-bellied Sapsucker (pg. 37) is smaller, and has red chin and forehead. Red-bellied Woodpecker (pg. 43) has a black-and-white zebra-striped back, red patch on head and lacks mustache. Flickers are the only brown-backed woodpeckers in Florida.

Stan's Notes: Populations swell in winter with northern migrants. The only woodpecker to regularly feed on ground, preferring ants and beetles. Produces antacid saliva to neutralize the acidic defense of ants. Male usually selects nest site, taking up to 12 days to excavate. Some have had success attracting flickers to nest boxes stuffed with sawdust. In flight, flashes golden yellow under wings and tail, and undulates deeply while giving a loud "wacka-wacka" call.

YEAR-ROUND

MOURNING DOVE
Zenaida macroura

Size: 12" (30 cm)

Male: Smooth fawn-colored dove with gray patch on the head. Iridescent pink, green around neck. Single black spot behind and below eyes. Black spots on wings and tail. Pointed wedge-shaped tail with white edges.

Female: similar to male, lacking iridescent pink and green neck feathers

Juvenile: spotted and streaked

Nest: platform; female and male build; 2 broods per year

Eggs: 2; white, unmarked

Incubation: 13-14 days; male and female incubate, the male during day, female at night

Fledging: 12-14 days; female and male feed young

Migration: non-migrator in Florida

Food: seeds, will come to seed feeders

Compare: The Eurasian Collared-Dove (pg. 251) is similar, but has a black collar. Similar to the White-winged Dove (pg. 243), but lacking a white edge on wings.

Stan's Notes: Name comes from its mournful cooing. Mates for life, roughly seven to ten years. A ground feeder, its head bobs as it walks. One of the few birds to drink without lifting head, same as Rock Dove. Parents feed the young a regurgitated liquid called crop-milk the first few days of life. Flimsy platform nest of twigs often falls apart in a storm. Wind rushing through wing feathers in flight creates a characteristic whistling sound.

CHUCK-WILL'S-WIDOW
Caprimulgus carolinensis

YEAR-ROUND
SUMMER

Size: 12" (30 cm)

Male: Mottled brown and black throughout with a thin light-tan necklace. Tiny bill and long rounded tail. White tail feathers are hidden.

Female: same as male, lacks the white tail feathers

Juvenile: same as adult

Nest: no nest; 1 brood per year

Eggs: 1-2; off-white with dark markings

Incubation: 20-24 days; female incubates

Fledging: 17-20 days; female feeds young

Migration: complete, to Central and South America

Food: insects, while in flight

Compare: Rarely seen due to its nocturnal behavior. Common Nighthawk (pg. 137) is smaller, has a white stripe across each wing (seen in flight) and a throat patch.

Stan's Notes: Usually is only heard and rarely seen. Gives a loud, repetitive, incessant call at night each spring and summer, "chuck-will's-widow." Most common in mixed oak and pine forest, where it lays its eggs directly on the ground, often in the same place each year. Will dart out from the nesting area (flush) if disturbed. Often roosts by perching parallel along the length of a branch, unlike other birds which roost diagonally on a branch. A tiny bill, but an enormous wide mouth (gape) to capture insects while in flight. Related to Whip-poor-will (not shown), which is more common in northern states. Year-round resident in southern Florida, but most migrate farther south.

YEAR-ROUND

PIED-BILLED GREBE
Podilymbus podiceps

Size: 13" (33 cm)

Male: Small brown water bird with a black chin and black ring around a thick, chicken-like ivory bill. White "puffy" under tail.

Female: same as male

Juvenile: paler than adult, with white spots and gray chest, belly and bill

Nest: floating platform; female and male build; 1 brood per year

Eggs: 5-7; bluish white, unmarked

Incubation: 22-24 days; female and male incubate

Fledging: 22-24 days; female and male feed young

Migration: complete, to southern states, Mexico and Central America, winters in Florida, non-migrator in Florida

Food: crayfish, aquatic insects, fish

Compare: The smallest brown water bird that dives underwater for long periods of time.

Stan's Notes: A very common water bird. Often seen diving for crayfish, aquatic insects and fish. It slowly sinks like a submarine when disturbed. Formerly called Hell-diver because of the length of time it stays submerged. Can surface far away from where it went under. Builds a platform nest on a floating mat in the water. Particularly sensitive to pollution. Adapted well to life on the water, with short wings, lobed toes and legs set close to the rear of body. While swimming is easy, it is very awkward on ground. The name "Grebe" probably came from the Old English word *krib*, meaning "crest," a reference to the Great Crested Grebe found in Europe.

159

WINTER

GREATER YELLOWLEGS
Tringa melanoleuca

Size: 14" (36 cm)

Male: A tall bird with bulbous head and long thin bill, slightly turned up. Gray streaking on chest and white belly. Long yellow legs.

Female: same as male

Juvenile: same as adult

Nest: ground; female builds; 1 brood per year

Eggs: 3-4; off-white with brown markings

Incubation: 22-23 days; female and male incubate

Fledging: 18-20 days; male and female feed young

Migration: complete, to southern states and South America

Food: small fish, aquatic insects

Compare: Nearly identical to the Lesser Yellowlegs (pg. 143), but larger, and with a longer and upturned bill.

Stan's Notes: A common shorebird that can be identified by the slightly upturned bill and long yellow legs. Often seen resting on one leg, its long legs carry it through deep water. Feeds by rushing forward through the water, plowing its bill or swinging it from side to side, catching small insects or fish. A skittish bird quick to give an alarm call, causing flocks to take flight. Quite often moves into the water prior to taking flight. Has a variety of "flight" notes that it gives when taking off. Nests on the ground near water on the northern tundra of Labrador and Newfoundland.

female

male pg. 17

BOAT-TAILED GRACKLE
Quiscalus major

YEAR-ROUND

Size: 14" (36 cm), female
16" (40 cm), male

Female: A golden brown chest and head with nearly black wings and tail, lacking iridescence.

Male: iridescent blue-black bird with a very long tail and brown or yellow eyes

Juvenile: similar to adult

Nest: cup; female builds; 2 broods per year

Eggs: 2-4; pale greenish blue, brown markings

Incubation: 13-15 days; female incubates

Fledging: 12-15 days; female feeds young

Migration: non-migrator, moves around to find food

Food: insects, berries, seeds, fish, visits feeders

Compare: Female Boat-tailed Grackle fairly distinctive and not confused with many other birds.

Stan's Notes: A bird of coastal saltwater and inland marshes. Boat-taileds north of Gainesville have yellow eyes, but in the rest of Florida the birds have brown eyes. A noisy bird that gives several harsh, high-pitched calls and several squeaks. Eats a wide variety of foods from grains to fish. Sometimes seen picking insects off the backs of cattle. Will also visit bird feeders. Makes a cup nest with mud or cow dung and grass. Nests in small colonies. Most nesting occurs from February through July and occasionally again from October to December.

breeding

winter pg. 255

displaying

WILLET
Catoptrophorus semipalmatus

YEAR-ROUND
WINTER

Size: 15" (38 cm)

Male: Brown breeding plumage with a brown bill and legs. White belly. Distinctive black and white wing lining pattern, seen in flight or during display.

Female: same as male

Juvenile: similar to breeding adult, only more tan in color than brown

Nest: ground; female builds; 1 brood per year

Eggs: 3-5; olive green with dark markings

Incubation: 24-28 days; male and female incubate

Fledging: unknown days; female and male feed young

Migration: complete, to South American coast, winters in coastal Florida

Food: aquatic insects

Compare: Slightly larger than the Greater Yellowlegs (pg. 161), which has yellow legs. Marbled Godwit (pg. 177) has two-toned, upturned bill. The breeding Short-billed Dowitcher (pg. 145) has yellow greenish legs.

Stan's Notes: Common along the coast in winter, many continue migrating though Florida to the coast of South America. It appears a rich, warm brown during breeding season and rather plain gray in winter, but always has a striking black and white wing pattern when seen in flight. Uses its black and white wing patches for displaying to mate. Named after the "pill-will-willet" call it gives while on its breeding ground. Gives a "kip-kip-kip" alarm call just as it takes flight. Nests along the coast, in western states and Canada.

female

male

WINTER

BLUE-WINGED TEAL
Anas discors

Size: 15-16" (38-40 cm)

Male: Small, plain-looking brown duck speckled with black. A gray head with a large white crescent-shaped mark at base of bill. Black tail with small white patch. Blue wing patch (speculum) usually only seen in flight.

Female: duller version of male, lacks facial crescent mark and white tail markings

Juvenile: same as female

Nest: ground; female builds; 1 brood per year

Eggs: 8-11; creamy white

Incubation: 23-27 days; female incubates

Fledging: 35-44 days; female feeds young

Migration: complete, to southern states and Central America

Food: aquatic plants, seeds, aquatic insects

Compare: Nearly half the size of the female Mallard (pg. 199). The female Blue-winged Teal is similar to the female Wood Duck (pg. 181), but lacks the Wood Duck's bright white eye ring and crest.

Stan's Notes: One of the most widespread and abundant winter ducks in Florida. Arrives in the state in August and leaves in April to May. Doesn't breed in Florida. Male leaves female near end of incubation. Female will perform distraction display to protect nest and young. Nest is built some distance from water. Planting crops and cultivating to pond edges are causing a decline in population.

male pg. 51

female

LESSER SCAUP
Aythya affinis

WINTER

Size: 16-17" (40-43 cm)

Female: Overall brown duck with dull white patch at base of light-gray bill. Yellow eyes.

Male: white and gray, the chest and head appear nearly black but head appears purple with green highlights in direct sun, yellow eyes

Juvenile: same as female

Nest: ground; female builds; 1 brood per year

Eggs: 8-14; olive buff without markings

Incubation: 22-28 days; female incubates

Fledging: 45-50 days; female teaches young to feed

Migration: complete, southern states, northern South America, Central America

Food: aquatic plants and insects

Compare: Similar size as the female Ring-necked Duck (pg. 173), but lacking the white ring around the bill. Look for the white patch at base of bill to help identify the female Lesser Scaup.

Stan's Notes: A common diving duck in the state. Often seen in large flocks numbering in the thousands on area lakes, ponds and sewage lagoons. Mostly seen during migrations in late February and in October. When seen in flight, note the bold white stripe under the wings. Has an interesting baby-sitting arrangement in which the young form groups tended by one to three adult females.

soaring

YEAR-ROUND

RED-SHOULDERED HAWK
Buteo lineatus

Size: 15-19" (38-48 cm); up to 3½-foot wingspan

Male: Reddish (cinnamon) head, shoulders, chest and belly. Wings and back are dark brown with white spots. Long tail with thin white bands and wide black bands. Obvious red wing linings, seen in flight.

Female: same as male

Juvenile: similar to adult, lacking the red color, white chest with dark spots

Nest: platform; female and male build; 1 brood per year

Eggs: 2-4; white with dark markings

Incubation: 27-29 days; female and male incubate

Fledging: 39-45 days; female and male feed young

Migration: non-migrator to partial migrator, winters in the U.S.

Food: reptiles, amphibians, large insects, birds

Compare: Sharp-shinned Hawk (pg. 249) is smaller and lacks Red-shouldered's reddish head and belly. The Red-tailed Hawk (pg. 187) is larger and has a white breast.

Stan's Notes: A common hawk of Florida forests, preferring to hunt along forest edges. Spots snakes, frogs, insects, an occasional small bird and other prey while perched. Often seen flapping with an alternating gliding pattern. Mates when 2 to 3 years old. Stays in same territory for many years. Nest building starts in February, with young leaving nests by June.

male pg. 53

female

WINTER

RING-NECKED DUCK
Aythya collaris

Size: 17" (43 cm)

Female: Mainly brown back with light brown sides, a gray face and dark brown crown. White eye ring extends into a line behind eyes. A white ring around bill. Top of head peaked.

Male: black head, chest and back, sides are gray to nearly white, bold white ring around bill and a second ring at the base of bill, top of head peaked

Juvenile: similar to adult

Nest: ground; female builds; 1 brood per year

Eggs: 8-10; olive gray to brown, unmarked

Incubation: 26-27 days; female incubates

Fledging: 49-56 days; female teaches young to feed

Migration: complete, to southern states, West Indies, Central America

Food: aquatic plants and insects

Compare: Female Lesser Scaup (pg. 169) is similar in size. Look for female Ring-necked's white ring around the bill.

Stan's Notes: One of the most abundant wintering ducks in the state. Usually seen in larger freshwater lakes rather than saltwater marshes. A diving duck, watch for it to dive underwater to forage for food. Takes to flight by springing up off water. Named "Ring-necked" due to a cinnamon-colored collar (nearly impossible to see in the field). Also known as Ring-billed Duck.

male pg. 55

female

HOODED MERGANSER
Lophodytes cucullatus

YEAR-ROUND
WINTER

Size: 16-19" (40-48 cm)

Female: Sleek brown and rust bird with a red head and ragged "hair" on the back of head. Gray body. Long, thin brown bill.

Male: same size and shape as female, but black back and rust sides, crest "hood" raises to reveal large white patch, long black bill

Juvenile: similar to female

Nest: cavity; female lines old woodpecker hole; 1 brood per year

Eggs: 10-12; white, unmarked

Incubation: 32-33 days; female incubates

Fledging: 71 days; female feeds young

Migration: complete, to Gulf coast and Mexico, non-migrator in central Florida

Food: small fish, aquatic insects

Compare: Very similar to, but smaller than, the female Red-breasted Merganser (pg. 195), which has a larger, lighter-colored bill. Larger than female Lesser Scaup (pg. 169), which has a dull white patch at base of bill.

Stan's Notes: A small diving bird of shallow-water ponds, sloughs, lakes and rivers. Rarely found away from wooded areas, where it nests in natural cavities or nest boxes. The female will "dump" eggs into other female Hooded Merganser nests, resulting in 20 to 25 eggs in some nests. Male can voluntarily raise and lower its crest to show off the large white patch on its head. Mergansers have been known to share a nest cavity with Wood Ducks sitting side by side.

MARBLED GODWIT
Limosa fedoa

WINTER

Size: 18" (45 cm)

Male: A tawny brown overall with a darker back. Long, two-toned and slightly upturned bill with black tip and pinkish base. Long gray legs. Cinnamon under wings, seen in flight.

Female: same as male

Juvenile: similar to adult

Nest: ground; the female and male build; 1 brood per year

Eggs: 3-5; olive green with dark markings

Incubation: 21-23 days; male and female incubate

Fledging: 20-21 days; female and male feed young

Migration: complete, East, Gulf and Central American coasts

Food: aquatic insects, snails, worms, leeches

Compare: Larger than the breeding Willet (pg. 165). Same size as Whimbrel (pg. 179), which has a down-curved bill, compared with the slightly upturned bill of the Godwit. Larger than the more common breeding Short-billed Dowitcher (pg. 145), which has a straight black bill.

Stan's Notes: A winter resident that is easily identified by its very long, two-toned, slightly upturned bill. Uses its bill to probe deep into sand and mud for insects. Usually feeds in mid-thigh water. In winter, prefers saltwater beaches and mud flats up and down the East coast. Returns to the Prairie Pothole regions of North Dakota and Canada for nesting. Nests in short grass prairie near wetlands.

WHIMBREL
Numenius phaeopus

Size: 18" (45 cm)

Male: Heavily streaked light-brown-to-gray bird. Long down-curved bill and multiple dark brown stripes on crown. Dark line though eyes. Light-gray-to-blue legs.

Female: same as male

Juvenile: similar to adult

Nest: ground; the female and male build; 1 brood per year

Eggs: 3-4; olive green with dark markings

Incubation: 27-28 days; male and female incubate

Fledging: 35-42 days; female and male feed young

Migration: complete, to Florida, coastal South America

Food: aquatic insects, snails, worms, leeches and berries

Compare: Larger than the breeding Willet (pg. 165). Same size as the Marbled Godwit (pg. 177), which has an upturned bill, compared with Whimbrel's down-curved bill. Larger than the more common Short-billed Dowitcher (pg. 145), which has a straight black bill.

Stan's Notes: A winter resident, easily identified by its very long down-curved bill and brown stripes on head. Uses its bill to probe deep into sand and mud for insects. Unlike the other shorebirds, berries become an important food source in summer. Is very vocal, giving single note whistles. Returns to tundra of northern Alaska for nesting. Doesn't breed until age 3 and has long-term pair bond. Adults leave breeding grounds up to two weeks before the young.

male pg. 273

female

WOOD DUCK
Aix sponsa

YEAR-ROUND
WINTER

Size: 17-20" (43-50 cm)

Female: A small brown dabbling duck. Bright white eye ring and a not-so-obvious crest. A blue patch on wing is often hidden.

Male: highly ornamented with a green head and crest patterned with white and black, rusty chest, white belly and red eyes

Juvenile: same as female

Nest: cavity; female lines old woodpecker cavity; 1 brood per year

Eggs: 10-15; creamy white, unmarked

Incubation: 28-36 days; female incubates

Fledging: 56-68 days; female teaches young to feed

Migration: complete, to southern states, non-migrator in Florida

Food: aquatic insects, plants, seeds

Compare: Smaller than the female Northern Shoveler (pg. 183) and lacks the long wide bill. Smaller than the female Mallard (pg. 199), which lacks Wood Duck's white eye ring.

Stan's Notes: A common duck of quiet, shallow backwater ponds. Nests in old woodpecker holes or in nest boxes. Often seen flying deep in forest or perched high on tree branches. Female takes flight with loud squealing call and enters nest cavity from full flight. Will lay eggs in a neighboring female nest (egg dumping), resulting in some clutches in excess of 20 eggs. Young remain in nest cavity only 24 hours after hatching, then jump from up to 30 feet to the ground or water to follow their mother, never returning to the nest.

male pg. 277

female

WINTER

NORTHERN SHOVELER
Anas clypeata

Size: 20" (50 cm)

Female: Medium-sized brown duck speckled with black. Blue wing patch. An extraordinarily large spoon-shaped bill, almost always held pointed toward the water.

Male: same spoon-shaped bill, iridescent green head, rusty sides and white breast

Juvenile: same as female

Nest: ground; female builds; 1 brood per year

Eggs: 9-12; olive, unmarked

Incubation: 22-25 days; female incubates

Fledging: 30-60 days; female leads young to food

Migration: complete, to southern states and Central America, winters in Florida

Food: aquatic insects, plants

Compare: Similar to female Mallard (pg. 199). Check for spoon-shaped bill. Larger size than the average female Wood Duck (pg. 181) and lacking the white eye ring.

Stan's Notes: One of several species of shoveler, so called because of the peculiarly shaped bill. The Northern Shoveler is the only species of these ducks in North America. A winter visitor, it arrives in Florida in September and leaves in April. Seen in small flocks of five to ten, swimming low in water with large bills always pointed toward the water, as if they're too heavy to lift. Feeds primarily by filtering tiny plants and insects from the water's surface with bill.

YEAR-ROUND

MOTTLED DUCK
Anas fulvigula

Size: 22" (56 cm)

Male: All-brown duck with a light tan neck and head. Bright yellow bill without markings. Wing patch (speculum) is blue (sometimes green) and outlined with black.

Female: same as male

Juvenile: same as adult

Nest: ground; female builds; 1 brood per year

Eggs: 5-10; off-white without markings

Incubation: 25-27 days; female incubates

Fledging: 60-70 days; female shows the young what to eat

Migration: non-migrator

Food: aquatic insects, crayfish, snails, grass, seeds

Compare: Similar to female Mallard (pg. 199), which has an orange bill with black markings. The female Mallard's blue speculum is outlined with white.

Stan's Notes: A year-round resident and widely hunted in Florida. It is most densely populated around the coast in both freshwater and saltwater marshes. Feeds on more insects and crayfish than the Mallard. Will breed with Mallards, producing hybrids. Mated pairs stay together all year, unlike Mallards. Young will scatter if mother feels threatened and gives an alarm call.

soaring

RED-TAILED HAWK
Buteo jamaicensis

YEAR-ROUND
WINTER

Size: 19-25" (48-63 cm); up to 4-foot wingspan

Male: Large hawk with amazing variety of colors from bird to bird, from chocolate brown to nearly all white. Often brown with a white breast and a distinctive brown belly band. Rust red tail usually only seen from above. Underside of wing is white with small dark patch on leading edge near shoulder.

Female: same as male, often larger

Juvenile: similar to adult, lacking a red tail, speckled chest

Nest: platform; male and female build; 1 brood per year

Eggs: 2-3; white, without markings or sometimes marked with brown

Incubation: 30-35 days; female and male incubate

Fledging: 45-46 days; male and female feed young

Migration: partial migrator, to southern states, non-migrator in Florida

Food: mice, birds, snakes, insects

Compare: Red-shouldered Hawk (pg. 171) and Sharp-shinned Hawk (pg. 249) are much smaller.

Stan's Notes: A common hawk of open country and cities in the state, often seen perched on freeway light posts. Look for it circling above open fields, searching for prey. Their large stick nests are commonly seen along roads in large trees. Stick nests are lined with finer material such as evergreen needles. Will return to the same nest site each year. Doesn't develop red tail until second year.

BARRED OWL
Strix varia

YEAR-ROUND

Size: 20-24" (50-60 cm)

Male: A chunky brown and gray owl with a large head and dark brown eyes. Dark horizontal barring on chest, and vertical streaking on the belly.

Female: same as male, only slightly larger

Juvenile: same as adult

Nest: cavity; no nesting material is brought in; 1 brood per year

Eggs: 2-3; white, unmarked

Incubation: 28-33 days; female incubates

Fledging: 42-44 days; female and male feed young

Migration: non-migrator

Food: mammals, small birds

Compare: It's our only owl with dark eyes. Lacks the "horns" of the Great Horned Owl (pg. 191) and ear tufts of the tiny Eastern Screech-Owl (pg. 237). The Eastern Screech-Owl and long-legged Burrowing Owl (pg. 139) are about half the size of the Barred Owl.

Stan's Notes: A very common owl that can often be seen hunting during the day. Prefers dense woodland with sparse undergrowth. Can be attracted by a simple nest box with a large opening, which is attached to a tree. The young will stay with the parents for up to four months after fledging. Often sounds like a dog barking just before giving an eight-hoot call that sounds like, "Who-cooks-for-you? Who-cooks-for-you?" The Great Horned Owl sounds like, "Hoo-hoo-hoo-hoooo!"

YEAR-ROUND

GREAT HORNED OWL
Bubo virginianus

Size: 20-25" (50-63 cm)

Male: A robust brown "horned" owl with bright yellow eyes and V-shaped white bib.

Female: same as male, only slightly larger

Juvenile: similar to adult

Nest: no nest; takes over the nests of crows, Great Blue Herons and hawks, or uses partial cavities; 1 brood per year

Eggs: 2; white, unmarked

Incubation: 26-30 days; female incubates

Fledging: 30-35 days; male and female feed young

Migration: non-migrator

Food: small mammals, birds, snakes, insects

Compare: The Barred Owl (pg. 189) has no "horns" and dark eyes. Over twice the size of the Eastern Screech-Owl (pg. 237).

Stan's Notes: The largest owl in Florida. "Ears" are actually tufts of feathers (horns) and have nothing to do with hearing. Not able to turn head all the way around. Wing feathers are ragged on the end, resulting in a silent flight. Eyelids close from the top down, like humans. Fearless, it is one of the few animals that will kill skunks and porcupines. Because of this, it is sometimes called Flying Tiger. A winter nesting bird in Florida, it lays eggs in January and February.

GLOSSY IBIS
Plegadis falcinellus

YEAR-ROUND
MIGRATION

Size: 23" (58 cm); up to 3-foot wingspan

Male: Chestnut brown head and neck. Iridescent green and blue wings and tail. Appears to be all dark brown from a distance. Very long, down-curved yellowish bill with blue facial skin near base. Long off-yellow legs.

Female: same as male

Juvenile: same as adult, lacking iridescent coloring

Nest: platform; female and male build; 1 brood per year

Eggs: 2-4; light blue without markings

Incubation: 20-21 days; female and male incubate

Fledging: 28-32 days; female and male feed young

Migration: partial migrator to non-migrator in Florida

Food: aquatic insects, crustaceans

Compare: One of two native ibis in Florida, the long down-curved bill helps identify them. The Glossy Ibis is brown and not confused with the White Ibis (pg. 315), which is all white.

Stan's Notes: A bird that seems to be on the increase in Florida. It prefers fresh water over salt water, with crayfish being a big part of the diet. From a distance the bird appears dark brown or nearly black, but when seen up close or through binoculars its iridescent green and bluish purple colors are amazing. Its long down-curved bill helps identify it in flight. Often seen flying in groups of 30 or more. Nests in large colonies with other wading birds.

male pg. 279

female

RED-BREASTED MERGANSER
Mergus serrator

WINTER

Size: 23" (58 cm)

Female: Overall brown-to-gray duck with a reddish head and crest. Long orange bill.

Male: shaggy green head and crest, a prominent white collar, black and white body, a long orange bill

Juvenile: similar to adult, male looks like the female at first, then changes

Nest: ground; female builds; 1 brood per year

Eggs: 5-10; olive green without markings

Incubation: 29-30 days; female incubates

Fledging: 55-65 days; female feeds young

Migration: complete, to the southern coastal states and Central America, winters in coastal Florida

Food: fish, aquatic insects

Compare: Very similar to, but larger than, the female Hooded Merganser (pg. 175), which has a smaller, darker bill than the bill of female Red-breasted Merganser.

Stan's Notes: A winter resident of coastal Florida. It is the most common of the wintering mergansers, arriving in late October and leaving in April. Most commonly seen along both coasts, but can also be seen in large inland freshwater lakes. A very fast flyer, often seen flying low and fast across the water. Needs a long take-off run to get airborne. Serrated bill helps it catch slippery fish. Doesn't breed before 2 years of age. Males abandon females just after eggs are laid. Females often share a nest. Nests across northern Canada and Alaska.

male pg. 257

female

NORTHERN HARRIER
Circus cyaneus

WINTER

Size: 24" (60 cm)

Female: A slim, low-flying hawk. Dark brown back with brown-streaked breast and belly. Large white rump patch and narrow black bands across tail. Tips of wings black.

Male: silver gray with large white rump patch and white belly, faint narrow bands across tail, tips of wings black

Juvenile: similar to female, with orange breast

Nest: platform; female and male build; 1 brood per year

Eggs: 4-8; bluish white, unmarked

Incubation: 31-32 days; female incubates

Fledging: 30-35 days; male and female feed young

Migration: complete, to southern states and Central America

Food: mice, snakes

Compare: Slimmer than Red-tailed Hawk (pg. 187). Look for black bands on tail and a white rump patch.

Stan's Notes: One of the easiest hawks to identify. Harriers glide just above the ground, following the contours of the land while searching for prey. Wings are held just above the horizontal position, tilting back and forth in the wind, similar to Turkey Vultures. Was formerly called Marsh Hawk due to its habit of hunting over marshes. Nests on the ground. At all ages, the Northern Harrier has distinctive owl-like face disks.

197

male pg. 281

female

MALLARD
Anas platyrhynchos

YEAR-ROUND

Size: 27-28" (69-71 cm)

Female: All brown with orange and black bill. Small blue and white wing mark (speculum).

Male: large, bulbous green head, white necklace, rust brown or chestnut chest, combination of gray and white on sides, yellow bill, legs and feet

Juvenile: same as female, but with yellow bill

Nest: ground; female builds; 1 brood per year

Eggs: 7-10; greenish to whitish, unmarked

Incubation: 26-30 days; female incubates

Fledging: 42-52 days; female leads young to food

Migration: complete, to southern states, non-migrator in Florida

Food: seeds, plants, aquatic insects, will come to ground feeders offering corn

Compare: Mottled Duck (pg. 185) is similar, but has a yellow bill, compared with the female Mallard's orange bill with black markings. The female Northern Shoveler (pg. 183) is smaller and has a large spoon-shaped bill. The female Wood Duck (pg. 181) is smaller and has a white eye ring.

Stan's Notes: A familiar duck of lakes and ponds. Will return to place of birth. The name "Mallard" comes from the Latin *masculus*, meaning "male," referring to the habit of males not taking part in raising ducklings. Both male and female have white tails and white underwings. Black central tail feathers of male curl upward.

WILD TURKEY
Meleagris gallopavo

YEAR-ROUND

Size: 36-48" (90-120 cm)

Male: Large, plump brown and bronze bird with striking blue and red bare head. Fan tail and long, straight black beard in center of chest. Spurs on legs.

Female: thinner and less striking than male, usually lacking breast beard

Juvenile: same as adult

Nest: ground; female builds; 1 brood per year

Eggs: 10-12; buff white with dull brown markings

Incubation: 27-28 days; female incubates

Fledging: 6-10 days; female leads young to food

Migration: non-migrator

Food: insects, seeds, fruit

Compare: This bird is distinctive and unlikely to be confused with others.

Stan's Notes: The largest game bird in Florida, and the bird from which the domestic turkey was bred. Nearly became our national bird, but lost by one vote to the Bald Eagle. Eliminated from many of the eastern states due to market hunting and the loss of habitat, they were reintroduced widely in the 1960-80s. Now populations are stable. Strong fliers, they can approach 60 mph. Able to fly straight up, then away. Eyesight three times better than in humans. Hearing is also excellent; able to hear competing males up to a mile away. Males hold "harems" of up to 20 females. Males are known as toms, females are hens and the young are called poults. At night, they roost in trees.

juvenile

breeding

chick-feeding adult

BROWN PELICAN
Pelecanus occidentalis

YEAR-ROUND

Size: 48" (120 cm); up to 9-foot wingspan

Male: Gray brown body, black belly, exceptionally long gray bill. Breeding adult has white or yellow head with dark chestnut hind neck. Adult that is feeding chicks (chick-feeding adult) has a speckled white head. A non-breeding adult has a white head and neck.

Female: similar to male

Juvenile: brown version of adult, not acquiring adult plumage until third year

Nest: platform; female and male build; 1 brood per year

Eggs: 2-4; white without markings

Incubation: 28-30 days; female and male incubate

Fledging: 71-86 days; female and male feed young

Migration: non-migrator in coastal Florida

Food: fish

Compare: An unmistakable bird in Florida.

Stan's Notes: A common bird of Florida, it is ironically on the endangered species list. Suffering from eggshell thinning in the 1970s due to DDT and other pesticides, the only population that remained viable was in Florida. It is now reestablishing along the East and Gulf coasts. Captures fish by diving headfirst into the ocean, opening its large bill and "netting" the fish with its gular pouch. Often seen sitting on posts around marinas. Nests in large colonies. Doesn't breed before 3 years of age, when it obtains its breeding plumage.

WINTER

RUBY-CROWNED KINGLET
Regulus calendula

Size: 4" (10 cm)

Male: Small, teardrop-shaped green-to-gray bird. Two white wing bars. Hidden ruby-colored crown. White eye ring.

Female: same as male, lacks ruby crown

Juvenile: same as adult

Nest: pendulous; female builds; 1 brood per year

Eggs: 4-5; white with brown markings

Incubation: 11-12 days; female incubates

Fledging: 11-12 days; female and male feed young

Migration: complete, to southern states, Mexico and Central America

Food: insects, berries

Compare: The female American Goldfinch (pg. 323) is larger, and shares same olive color and unmarked breast. Look for the white eye ring of Ruby-crowned Kinglet.

Stan's Notes: The second smallest bird in the state, it takes a quick eye to see the male's ruby crown. Most commonly seen during the spring and autumn migrations, look for it flitting around thick shrubs low to the ground. Builds an unusual pendulous (sac-like) nest, intricately woven and decorated on the outside with colored lichens and mosses stuck together with spider webs. The nest is suspended from a branch overlapped by leaves, usually hung high in mature trees. The name "Kinglet" comes from the Anglo-Saxon *cyning*, or "king," referring to its ruby crown, and the diminutive suffix "let," meaning "small."

BROWN-HEADED NUTHATCH
Sitta pusilla

YEAR-ROUND

Size: 4½" (11 cm)

Male: Gray back. Brown cap bordered by a black line that extends through eyes. A dull white chin, chest and belly. Pale gray spot at the nape of neck, hard to see from a distance.

Female: same as male

Juvenile: same as adult

Nest: cavity; the female and male build; 1 brood per year

Eggs: 3-5; white with dark markings

Incubation: 12-14 days; female incubates

Fledging: 18-19 days; female and male feed young

Migration: non-migrator

Food: insects, seeds, comes to seed feeders

Compare: Carolina Chickadee (pg. 209) is similar in size, but has a black cap, compared with the brown cap of the Nuthatch.

Stan's Notes: A tiny bird of open pine forest in Florida. Like other nuthatches, it feeds by creeping up and down twigs and trunks of trees, looking for insects and insect eggs. Works hard to remove seeds from cones on evergreen trees. Has been known to cache pine seeds for later consumption. Will visit seed feeders. A cavity nester, it will excavate its own cavity, take an abandoned woodpecker home or use a nest box. Occasionally an unmated male helper attends to a mated female on the nest. Will stay with mate nearly all year, defending a very small territory.

CAROLINA CHICKADEE
Poecile carolinensis

Size: 5" (13 cm)

Male: Mostly gray bird with a black cap and chin. White face and chest with tan belly. Darker gray tail.

Female: same as male

Juvenile: same as adult

Nest: cavity; female and male build or excavate; 1-2 broods per year

Eggs: 5-7; white with reddish brown markings

Incubation: 11-12 days; female and male incubate

Fledging: 13-17 days; female and male feed young

Migration: non-migrator

Food: insects, seeds, fruit, comes to seed and suet feeders

Compare: Similar in size to Brown-headed Nuthatch (pg. 207), but lacking a brown cap. Tufted Titmouse (pg. 213) has an erect crest, and lacks the black cap and chin.

Stan's Notes: A common bird of Florida. Can be attracted with a nest box with a 1¼-inch entrance hole. Females will give a loud snake-like hiss when disturbed on the nest. Often seen with other birds (mixed flock) during the winter. A friendly bird that can be tamed and hand fed. The Carolina Chickadee's song is a high, fast "chick-a-dee-dee-dee."

male

female

YELLOW-RUMPED WARBLER
Dendroica coronata

WINTER

Size: 5-6" (13-15 cm)

Male: Slate gray bird with black mask and chest. Yellow patch on the head, flanks and rump. White chin and belly. Two white wing bars.

Female: similar to male, duller color, mostly brown and white with matching yellow patches

Juvenile: similar to female

Nest: cup; female builds; 2 broods per year

Eggs: 4-5; white with brown markings

Incubation: 12-13 days; female incubates

Fledging: 10-12 days; female and male feed young

Migration: complete, to southern states, Mexico and Central America

Food: insects, berries, rarely comes to suet feeders

Compare: Similar to other warblers, look for a combination of yellow patches on head, flanks and rump. Palm Warbler (pg. 327) has a yellow throat and chestnut-colored crown. The Common Yellowthroat (pg. 325) has yellow breast, compared with the Yellow-rumped's spots of yellow.

Stan's Notes: One of the most common winter warblers. Formerly called Myrtle Warbler because it was thought to eat the berries of the myrtle. Sometimes called Butter-butts due to the yellow patch on rump. Males molt to a dull color similar to females each winter, retaining yellow patches. Familiar call is a robust "chip."

TUFTED TITMOUSE
Baeolophus bicolor

YEAR-ROUND

Size: 6" (15 cm)

Male: Slate gray bird with a white chest and belly. Pointed crest. Flanks are washed in a rusty brown. Gray legs and dark eyes.

Female: same as male

Juvenile: same as adult

Nest: cavity, takes over former woodpecker hole; female builds; 2 broods per year

Eggs: 5-7; white with brown markings

Incubation: 13-14 days; female incubates

Fledging: 15-18 days; female and male feed young

Migration: non-migrator

Food: insects, seeds, fruit, will come to seed and suet feeders

Compare: Closely related to the Carolina Chickadee (pg. 209), but is slightly larger. Chickadee lacks crest of the Tufted Titmouse.

Stan's Notes: Is well known for its quickly repeated "peter-peter-peter" call. Prefix "Tit" comes from a Scandinavian word meaning "little." Suffix "mouse" is derived from the Old English word *mase*, meaning "bird." Simply translated, it is "a small bird." Notorious for pulling hair from sleeping dogs, cats and squirrels to line their nests. Attracted with nest boxes. Usually seen only one or two at a time. Male feeds female during courtship and nesting.

breeding
pg. 115

winter

LEAST SANDPIPER
Calidris minutilla

MIGRATION
WINTER

Size: 6" (15 cm)

Male: Dull yellow legs. Short, down-curved black bill. White belly. Winter plumage is overall gray to light brown with a distinct brown breast band and light gray eyebrows.

Female: same as male

Juvenile: similar to winter adult, but buff brown and lacking the breast band

Nest: ground; the male and female build; 1 brood per year

Eggs: 3-4; olive with dark markings

Incubation: 19-23 days; male and female incubate

Fledging: 25-28 days; male and female feed young

Migration: complete, to southern coastal states and Central America

Food: insects, aquatic insects, seeds

Compare: The smallest of sandpipers. Often confused with winter Western Sandpiper (pg. 219) and Semipalmated Sandpiper (pg. 217), Least Sandpiper's yellow legs differentiate it from other tiny sandpipers. The short, thin, down-curved bill also helps to identify.

Stan's Notes: Winters all along the southern coastal states from Florida to California. It's the smallest of the peeps (sandpipers) that nest on the tundra in northern parts of Canada and Alaska. The yellow legs can be difficult to see in water, poor light or if covered with mud. Prefers the grassy flats of both saltwater and freshwater ponds. A tame sandpiper that can be approached without scaring.

breeding

winter

SEMIPALMATED SANDPIPER
Calidris pusilla

MIGRATION

Size: 6" (15 cm)

Male: Plump gray shorebird with black legs and a short, straight, blunt-tipped black bill. Has grayish brown head, neck and back, white chest and eyebrows in the winter plumage. Breeding (usually seen in the Arctic) has a brown head, some black and brown spots on the back, and a white belly.

Female: same as male

Juvenile: overall gray-brown with black spots

Nest: ground; the male and female build; 1 brood per year

Eggs: 2-4; light yellow with brown markings

Incubation: 18-22 days; male and female incubate

Fledging: 18-20 days; male and female feed young

Migration: complete, to Bahamas and northern South America

Food: aquatic insects

Compare: Much darker gray than the winter plumage of Sanderling (pg. 229). Look for black legs and shorter bill of the Semipalmated.

Stan's Notes: The most common shorebird in Florida. Seen during spring migration (mid-May to early June) and fall migration (July to August). Few individuals stay year-round. Males do most of the care of young after hatching, since females abandon their families about two to three days after eggs hatch. Will retain same mate for several years. Nests in northern Canada and Alaska.

breeding
pg. 117

winter

WESTERN SANDPIPER
Calidris mauri

MIGRATION
WINTER

Size: 6½" (16 cm)

Male: Black legs. Narrow bill that droops near tip. Winter plumage is dull gray to light brown overall with white belly and eyebrows.

Female: same as male

Juvenile: similar to breeding adult, bright buff brown on back only

Nest: ground; the male and female build; 1 brood per year

Eggs: 2-4; light brown with dark markings

Incubation: 20-22 days; male and female incubate

Fledging: 19-21 days; male and female feed young

Migration: complete, to southern coastal states and Central America

Food: insects, aquatic insects

Compare: Very often confused with the winter Least Sandpiper (pg. 215) and the Semipalmated Sandpiper (pg. 217). Look for black legs to differentiate from Least Sandpiper. Western has a longer bill that droops slightly at tip.

Stan's Notes: A winter resident of Florida, it also winters all along the southern coastal states from Florida to California. Nests on the ground in large "loose" colonies on the tundra of northern coastal Alaska. Adults leave breeding grounds several weeks before the young. Some will obtain breeding plumage before leaving Florida in spring. Feeds in deeper water than the Semipalmated Sandpiper.

YEAR-ROUND

COMMON GROUND-DOVE
Columbina passerina

Size: 6½" (16 cm)

Male: A very small dove with a short tail and a unique scalloped effect on head and breast. Black-tipped reddish-orange bill. Slate gray crown and pinkish-gray underside. Bright chestnut wings, seen only in flight.

Female: similar to male, but grayer and has a more uniform color

Juvenile: similar to adult

Nest: ground; female and male build; 2-4 broods per year

Eggs: 2-4; white without markings

Incubation: 12-14 days; female and male incubate

Fledging: 10-11 days; female and male feed young

Migration: non-migrator

Food: seeds, berries, will come to seed feeders

Compare: Mourning Dove (pg. 155) is twice the size of Common Ground-Dove. Lacks Ground-Dove's scalloped effect and its black-tipped reddish-orange bill.

Stan's Notes: The smallest dove in Florida, it was formerly called Eastern Ground Dove. Known to continually bob its head, and is often seen in pairs. Unafraid of humans, it spends most of its time on the ground. While it usually nests on the ground, it will sometimes build a flimsy nest in a shrub or take an abandoned nest low in a tree. Found in open dry woodland, old fields and pastures.

EASTERN PHOEBE
Sayornis phoebe

WINTER

Size:	7" (18 cm)
Male:	Gray bird with dark wings, light olive green belly and a thin dark bill.
Female:	same as male
Juvenile:	same as adult
Nest:	cup; female builds; 2 broods per year
Eggs:	4-5; white, unmarked
Incubation:	15-16 days; female incubates
Fledging:	15-16 days; male and female feed young
Migration:	complete, to southern states and Mexico
Food:	insects
Compare:	Like most other olive gray birds, it is hard to distinguish identifying markings. Eastern Phoebe lacks any white eye ring. Easier to identify by well-enunciated song, "fee-bee," or characteristic of hawking for insects.

Stan's Notes: A sparrow-sized bird often seen on the end of a dead branch. It sits waiting for a passing insect, flies out to catch it and then returns to the same branch, a process called hawking. Has a habit of pumping and spreading its tail when perched. Will build nest under the eaves of a house, under a bridge or in culverts. The nest, made of mud, grass and moss, is lined with hair and feathers. The name is derived from its characteristic song, "fee-bee," which is repeated over and over from the tops of dead branches.

EASTERN KINGBIRD
Tyrannus tyrannus

SUMMER

Size: 8" (20 cm)

Male: Mostly black gray bird with white belly and chin. Black head and tail with a distinctive white band across the end of the tail. Has a concealed red crown that is rarely seen.

Female: same as male

Juvenile: same as adult

Nest: cup; male and female build; 1 brood a year

Eggs: 3-4; white with brown markings

Incubation: 16-18 days; female incubates

Fledging: 16-18 days; female and male feed young

Migration: complete, to Central and South America

Food: insects, fruit

Compare: Rarely confused with other birds. Medium-sized bird, smaller than American Robin (pg. 239). Look for the white band along the end of the tail to identify.

Stan's Notes: A common bird of open fields and pastures. Acting unafraid of other birds and chasing the larger ones, it is perceived as having an attitude. Bold behavior gave rise to its common name, King. Perches on tall branches, watching for insects. After flying out to catch them, returns to the same perch, a technique called hawking. Male and female return to mating ground and defend a territory together.

GREAT CRESTED FLYCATCHER
Myiarchus crinitus

Size: 8" (20 cm)

Male: Gray head with prominent crest. Gray back and throat with bright yellow belly, yellow extending under reddish brown tail. Lower bill is yellow at base.

Female: same as male

Juvenile: same as adult

Nest: cavity; the female and male build; 1 brood per year

Eggs: 4-6; white or buff with brown markings

Incubation: 13-15 days; female incubates

Fledging: 14-21 days; female and male feed young

Migration: complete, to Mexico and Central America, non-migrator in southern tip of Florida

Food: insects, fruit

Compare: The Eastern Kingbird (pg. 225) has a white band across the tail. Similar to the Eastern Phoebe (pg. 223), but the Flycatcher has an obvious crest, and yellow chest and belly.

Stan's Notes: One of the largest flycatchers in Florida that has a prominent crest. A common bird of almost any wooded area, it lives high up in trees, rarely coming to ground. Often heard before seen. Feeds by gleaning insects from leaves of trees. Nests in old woodpecker holes, but can be attracted to a nest box placed high up in a tree with an entrance hole of 1½-2½ inches. Often stuffs nest with a collection of fur, feathers, string and snakeskins. Breeds throughout the state.

breeding
pg. 129

winter

SANDERLING
Calidris canutus

WINTER

Size: 8" (20 cm)

Male: Black legs and bill. Winter plumage head and back are gray and belly is white. White wing stripe, seen only in flight. During the winter it's the lightest-colored sandpiper on the beach.

Female: same as male

Juvenile: spotty black on head and back, with white belly, black legs and bill

Nest: ground; male builds; 1-2 broods per year

Eggs: 3-4; greenish-olive with brown markings

Incubation: 24-30 days; male and female incubate

Fledging: 16-17 days; female and male feed young

Migration: partial migrator to complete, to West Indies and East, Gulf and South American coasts

Food: insects

Compare: Same size as the winter plumage Spotted Sandpiper (pg. 127).

Stan's Notes: One of the most common shorebirds in the state, but mostly seen in gray winter plumage from August to April. Can be seen in groups on sandy beaches, running out with each retreating wave to feed. Look for a flash of white on wings when in flight. Occasionally the female will mate with several males (polyandry), resulting in males and the female incubating separate nests. Both sexes will perform a distraction display if threatened. Nests in the Arctic tundra. Declining in populations. Surveys show a greater than 80 percent decline in numbers since the 1970s.

winter

breeding
pg. 131

DUNLIN
Calidris alpina

WINTER

Size: 8-9" (20-22.5 cm)

Male: Black legs. Stout bill curved slightly downward at the tip. Winter has a grayish brown back with light gray chest and white belly.

Female: slightly larger than male, with longer bill

Juvenile: slightly rusty back with spotty chest

Nest: ground; the male and female build; 1 brood per year

Eggs: 2-4; an olive-buff or a blue-green with red-brown markings

Incubation: 21-22 days; male and female incubate, the male during day, female at night

Fledging: 19-21 days; male feeds young, female often leaves before young fledge

Migration: complete, to southern coastal states and the Central American coast, winters in coastal Florida

Food: insects

Compare: Similar size as winter Sanderling (pg. 229), but the winter Dunlin has a longer down-turned bill and is an overall darker gray.

Stan's Notes: Usually seen in gray winter plumage from August to early May. Breeding plumage is more common in spring. Flights include heights of 100 feet with brief gliding alternating with shallow flutters, and rhythmic, repeating song. In flight, look for dark center on rump. Huge flocks fly synchronously, with birds twisting and turning, flashing their light and dark undersides. Males tend to fly farther south than females in winter. Doesn't nest in Florida.

GRAY CATBIRD
Dumetella carolinensis

YEAR-ROUND
WINTER

Size: 9" (22.5 cm)

Male: Handsome slate-gray bird with black crown and a long, thin black bill. Often seen with its tail lifted, exposing a chestnut-colored patch under tail.

Female: same as male

Juvenile: same as adult

Nest: cup; female and male build; 2 broods a year

Eggs: 4-6; blue green, unmarked

Incubation: 12-13 days; female incubates

Fledging: 10-11 days; female and male feed young

Migration: complete, to southern states

Food: insects, fruit

Compare: Larger than Eastern Phoebe (pg. 223), it lacks the Phoebe's olive belly. Similar size as Eastern Kingbird (pg. 225), but it lacks the Kingbird's white belly and white tail band.

Stan's Notes: A secretive bird that the Chippewa Indians named Bird That Cries With Grief due to its raspy call. The call sounds like a house cat's mewing, hence its common name. It often mimics other birds, rarely repeating the same phrases. Will only nest in thick shrubs and is more often heard than seen. Quickly flies back into the shrubs when approached. If a cowbird introduces an egg into a catbird nest, the catbird will quickly break it, then eject it.

YEAR-ROUND

LOGGERHEAD SHRIKE
Lanius ludovicianus

Size: 9" (22.5 cm)

Male: A gray head and back with black wings and mask across the eyes. A white chin, chest and belly. Black tail, legs and feet. Black bill with hooked tip. White wing patches, seen in flight.

Female: same as male

Juvenile: dull version of adult

Nest: cup; the male and female build; 1-2 broods per year

Eggs: 4-7; off-white with dark markings

Incubation: 16-17 days; female incubates

Fledging: 17-21 days; female and male feed young

Migration: complete, to southern states and Mexico, winters in Florida

Food: insects, lizards, small mammals, frogs

Compare: The Northern Mockingbird (pg. 241) has a similar color pattern, but lacks the black mask of the Loggerhead. Shrike is stockier than the Mockingbird and perches in more open places.

Stan's Notes: The Loggerhead is a songbird that acts like a bird of prey. Known for skewering prey on barbed wire fences, thorns and other sharp objects to store or hold still while tearing apart to eat, hence its other name, Butcher Bird. Feet are too weak to hold prey while eating. During the winter, Loggerheads from northern states enter Florida, swelling populations. On the decline overall due to pesticides killing its major food source–grasshoppers.

YEAR-ROUND

EASTERN SCREECH-OWL
Otus asio

Size: 9" (22.5 cm)

Male: Small "eared" owl that occurs in one of two permanent color morphs. Is either mottled with gray and white, or is red brown with white. Bright yellow eyes.

Female: same as male

Juvenile: lighter gray than adult, may lack ear tufts

Nest: cavity; former woodpecker cavity; 1 brood per year

Eggs: 4-5; white, unmarked

Incubation: 25-26 days; female incubates, male feeds female during incubation

Fledging: 26-27 days; male and female feed young

Migration: non-migrator

Food: large insects, small mammals, birds, snakes

Compare: The only small owl in the state with ear tufts. Can be gray or rust colored.

Stan's Notes: A common owl active at dusk and during the night. Excellent hearing and eyesight. Seldom gives a screeching call; more commonly gives a tremulous, descending whiny trill that sounds like it came from the sound track of a scary movie. Will nest in wooden nest box. Often seen sunning themselves at nest box holes during winter. Male and female roost together at night, and are thought to mate for life. Different colorations are called morphs. Gray morph more common than red.

male

female

YEAR-ROUND
WINTER

AMERICAN ROBIN
Turdus migratorius

Size: 9-11" (22.5-28 cm)

Male: A familiar gray bird with a rusty red chest, a nearly black head and tail, and black streaks on white chin. White eye ring.

Female: similar to male, but has a gray head and a duller chest

Juvenile: similar to female, but has a speckled chest and brown back

Nest: cup; female builds with help from the male; 2 broods per year

Eggs: 4-7; pale blue, unmarked

Incubation: 12-14 days; female incubates

Fledging: 14-16 days; female and male feed young

Migration: complete, to southern states and Central America, small percentage non-migrator

Food: insects, fruit, berries, worms

Compare: Familiar bird to all.

Stan's Notes: A common winter resident of Florida. Can be heard singing all night long during spring. Most people don't realize how easy it is to tell the difference between the male and female robin. Look for the male's dark, nearly black head and brick-red chest, compared with the female's gray head and dull red chest. Robins are not listening for worms when they cock their heads to one side or the other. They are looking with eyes that are placed far back on the sides of their heads. A very territorial bird. Often seen fighting its own reflection in windows.

displaying

NORTHERN MOCKINGBIRD
Mimus polyglottos

Size: 10" (25 cm)

Male: Silvery gray head and back with light gray chest and belly. White wing patches, seen in flight or during display. Tail mostly black with white outer tail feathers. Black bill.

Female: same as male

Juvenile: overall dull gray, a heavily streaked chest, gray bill

Nest: cup; female and male build; 2 broods per year, sometimes more

Eggs: 3-5; blue green with brown markings

Incubation: 12-13 days; female incubates

Fledging: 11-13 days; female and male feed young

Migration: non-migrator

Food: insects, fruit

Compare: The Gray Catbird (pg. 233) is a slate gray and lacks the Mockingbird's wing patches. Look for Mockingbird to spread its wings, flash its white wing patches and wag its tail from side to side.

Stan's Notes: Very animated, male and female perform elaborate mating dances by facing each other, heads and tails erect. They run toward each other, flashing white wing patches, and then retreat to nearby cover. Thought to also flash wing patches to scare up insects when hunting. Known to imitate other birds (vocal mimicry), hence its common name. Young males often sing at night.

YEAR-ROUND
MIGRATION

WHITE-WINGED DOVE
Zenaida asiatica

Size: 11" (28 cm)

Male: A light gray to brown with a conspicuous white edge on the wings. Small black dash under cheeks. Surrounding bright red eyes are vivid blue eye rings. In flight, a white patch across the middle of the wings with black wing tips.

Female: same as male

Juvenile: similar to adult

Nest: platform; the female and male build; 2-3 broods per year

Eggs: 2-4; white without markings

Incubation: 13-14 days; female and male incubate

Fledging: 13-16 days; female and male feed young

Migration: non-migrator to partial migrator

Food: seeds, fruit, will come to seed feeders

Compare: Slightly smaller than the Mourning Dove (pg. 155), which lacks the white line on closed wings, and white and black pattern of the White-winged Dove in flight.

Stan's Notes: Very similar to the Mourning Dove in behavior and appearance. Feeds on the ground, pecking at seeds and tiny grains of rock to aid digestion. Parents feed young a regurgitated liquid called crop-milk the first few days of life. Males use their white and black wing coloration to display to mates. May nest along or in large colonies. A year-round resident in most of Florida but is not native, being introduced during the 1950s when captive birds were released near Homestead. Has a distinctive "coo-cuk-ca-roo" call.

breeding
pg. 145

winter

YEAR-ROUND

SHORT-BILLED DOWITCHER
Limnodromus griseus

Size: 11" (28 cm)

Male: Long, straight black bill. Off-white eyebrow stripe. Dull-yellow-to-green legs and feet. Winter plumage back and wings are gray to light brown and belly is white.

Female: same as male

Juvenile: similar to winter adult

Nest: ground; the female and male build; 1 brood per year

Eggs: 3-4; olive green with dark markings

Incubation: 20-21 days; male and female incubate

Fledging: 25-27 days; male and female feed young

Migration: complete, to the southern coastal states and Central America, winters in coastal Florida

Food: insects, snails, worms, leeches, seeds

Compare: The winter Black-bellied Plover (pg. 247) is similar in size, but has a tiny bill, compared with Dowitcher's long bill. Smaller than the winter Willet (pg. 255), which has shorter bill, and bold black and white wing linings.

Stan's Notes: A common year-round resident found along both Florida coasts and inland on freshwater lakes and marshes. With a rapid probing action like a sewing machine, uses its long straight bill to probe deep into sand and mud for insects. Can be seen with the less common Long-billed Dowitcher (not shown), but it's hard to tell the two apart.

245

breeding
pg. 47

winter

MIGRATION
WINTER

BLACK-BELLIED PLOVER
Pluvialis squatarola

Size: 11-12" (28-30 cm)

Male: Black legs and bill. Plumage in the winter is a uniform light gray with dark, nearly black streaks. White chest and belly. Faint white eyebrow mark.

Female: less black on chest and belly than male

Juvenile: grayer than adult, with much less black

Nest: ground; the male and female build; 1 brood per year

Eggs: 3-4; pinkish or greenish with black-brown markings

Incubation: 26-27 days; male and female incubate, the male during day, female at night

Fledging: 35-45 days; male feeds young, young learn quickly to feed themselves

Migration: complete, to the West Indies, East and Gulf coasts, coastal South America

Food: insects

Compare: Slightly larger than winter Dunlin (pg. 231) and lacking its long downward-curved bill.

Stan's Notes: The males perform a "butterfly" courtship flight to attract females. Female leaves male and young about 12 days after the eggs hatch. Breeds at 3 years of age. Arrivals start in July and August (fall migration). In flight, in any plumage, Plover displays a white rump and stripe on the wings with black axillaries (armpits). Often darts across ground to grab an insect and run.

soaring

juvenile

SHARP-SHINNED HAWK
Accipiter striatus

WINTER

Size: 10-14" (25-36 cm)

Male: Small woodland hawk with gray back and head, and rusty red breast. Long tail with several dark tail bands, widest band at end of squared-off tail. Red eyes.

Female: same as male, only larger

Juvenile: same size as adult, with a brown back and heavily streaked breast, yellow eyes

Nest: platform; female builds; 1 brood per year

Eggs: 4-5; white with brown markings

Incubation: 32-35 days; female incubates

Fledging: 24-27 days; female and male feed young

Migration: complete, to southern states, Mexico and Central America, winters in Florida

Food: birds, small mammals

Compare: Red-shouldered Hawk (pg. 171) is larger and lacks the Sharp-shinned's gray back.

Stan's Notes: A common hawk of backyards and woodland, often seen swooping in on birds visiting feeders. Short rounded wings and long tail allow this hawk to navigate through thick stands of trees in pursuit of prey. Common name comes from the sharp keel on the leading edge of its "shin," although it is actually below rather than above the bird's ankle on the tarsus bone of foot. The tarsus in most birds is round.

EURASIAN COLLARED-DOVE
Streptopelia decaocto

Size: 12½" (32 cm)

Male: Head, neck, chest and belly are pale gray to a light tan. Slightly darker back, wings and tail. Black collar is bordered with white and extends around the nape of neck.

Female: same as male

Juvenile: similar to adult

Nest: platform; the female and male build; 2-3 broods per year

Eggs: 3-5; creamy white without markings

Incubation: 12-14 days; female and male incubate

Fledging: 12-14 days; female and male feed young

Migration: non-migrator

Food: seeds

Compare: Slightly larger and lighter in color than the Mourning Dove (pg. 155). Look for the black collar to help identify.

Stan's Notes: A non-native dove that spread to Florida in the early 1980s after being introduced to the Bahamas. Is now expanding throughout North America, having reached the northern states beginning in the late 1990s. Predicted to spread throughout North America in the same way it spread throughout Europe from the Middle East. Nearly identical to the Ringed Turtle-Dove, a common pet bird.

ROCK DOVE
Columba livia

YEAR-ROUND

Size: 13" (33 cm)

Male: No set color pattern. Gray to white, patches of iridescent greens and blues, usually with a light rump patch.

Female: same as male

Juvenile: same as adult

Nest: platform; female builds; 3-4 broods a year

Eggs: 1-2; white, unmarked

Incubation: 18-20 days; female and male incubate

Fledging: 25-26 days; female and male feed young

Migration: non-migrator

Food: seeds

Compare: Larger than light-brown-colored Mourning Dove (pg. 155).

Stan's Notes: Also known as Domestic Pigeon, it was introduced to North America from Europe by the early settlers. Most common around cities and barnyards, where it scratches for seeds. The wide color variation comes from years of selective breeding while in captivity. Parents feed young a regurgitated liquid called crop-milk the first few days of life. One of the few birds that can drink without tilting its head back. Nests under bridges, on buildings, balconies, barns and sheds. Once poisoned as a "nuisance city bird," many cities have Peregrine Falcons that feed on Rock Doves, keeping their numbers in check.

breeding
pg. 165

displaying

winter

YEAR-ROUND
WINTER

WILLET
Catoptrophorus semipalmatus

Size: 15" (38 cm)

Male: Winter plumage is gray with a gray bill and legs. White belly. A distinctive black and white wing lining pattern, seen in flight or during display.

Female: same as male

Juvenile: similar to breeding adult, only more tan in color than brown

Nest: ground; female builds; 1 brood per year

Eggs: 3-5; olive green with dark markings

Incubation: 24-28 days; male and female incubate

Fledging: unknown days; female and male feed young

Migration: complete, to South American coast, winters in coastal Florida

Food: aquatic insects

Compare: Very similar to the light-gray winter Short-billed Dowitcher (pg. 245), which has a longer bill, yellow greenish legs and rarely looks up from its constant feeding. Slightly larger than Greater Yellowlegs (pg. 161), which has yellow legs.

Stan's Notes: Common along the coast in winter, many continue migrating though Florida to the coast of South America. In any plumage, always has a striking black and white wing pattern when seen in flight. Uses its black and white wing patches for displaying to mate. Named after the "pill-will-willet" call it gives while on its breeding ground. Gives a "kip-kip-kip" alarm call just as it takes flight. Nests along the coast, in western states and Canada.

male

female pg. 197

NORTHERN HARRIER
Circus cyaneus

WINTER

Size: 24" (60 cm)

Male: A slim, low-flying hawk. Silver gray with a large white rump patch and a white belly. Faint narrow bands across the tail. Tips of wings black.

Female: dark brown back, a brown-streaked breast and belly, large white rump patch, narrow black bands across tail, tips of wings black

Juvenile: similar to female, with orange breast

Nest: platform; female and male build; 1 brood per year

Eggs: 4-8; bluish white, unmarked

Incubation: 31-32 days; female incubates

Fledging: 30-35 days; male and female feed young

Migration: complete, to southern states and Central America

Food: mice, snakes

Compare: Slimmer than Red-tailed Hawk (pg. 187). Look for black bands on tail and a white rump patch.

Stan's Notes: One of the easiest hawks to identify. Harriers glide just above the ground, following the contours of the land while searching for prey. Wings are held just above the horizontal position, tilting back and forth in the wind, similar to Turkey Vultures. Was formerly called Marsh Hawk due to its habit of hunting over marshes. Nests on the ground. At all ages, the Northern Harrier has distinctive owl-like face disks.

juvenile

YEAR-ROUND
SUMMER

YELLOW-CROWNED NIGHT-HERON
Nyctanassa violacea

Size: 24" (60 cm); up to 3½-foot wingspan

Male: Stocky gray heron with a black head, white crown and cheek patch. Dark thick bill and yellow legs. During breeding season, crown acquires a yellow hue.

Female: same as male

Juvenile: brown with white streaks and a dark bill, green legs

Nest: platform; female and male build; 1 brood per year

Eggs: 4-6; light blue without markings

Incubation: 21-25 days; female and male incubate

Fledging: 21-25 days; female and male feed young

Migration: non-migrator to partial migrator

Food: aquatic insects, fish, crustaceans

Compare: One of many heron species in Florida. The distinctive patterned black and white head makes this heron easy to identify.

Stan's Notes: It hunts at night, as the common name implies, but can also be active during the day. Found in coastal mangroves to interior swamps, it often hunts fiddler crabs and crayfish. It is not uncommon for it to nest in large heron rookeries, and sometimes will nest by itself or in small colonies. Usually seen solitary or in small groups. During the breeding season, the crown will acquire a yellow hue.

YEAR-ROUND

CANADA GOOSE
Branta canadensis

Size: 25-43" (63-109 cm)

Male: Large gray goose with black neck and head, with a white chin or cheek strap.

Female: same as male

Juvenile: same as adult

Nest: ground; female builds; 1 brood per year

Eggs: 5-10; white, unmarked

Incubation: 25-30 days; female incubates

Fledging: 42-55 days; male and female teach young to feed

Migration: partial migrator, to southern states, non-migrator

Food: aquatic plants, insects, seeds

Compare: A large goose that is hardly ever confused with any other bird.

Stan's Notes: Once not too common, they have adapted to our changed environment very well. Adults will mate for many years, and will only start to breed in their third year. The males often act as sentinels, standing on the edge of the group and bobbing their heads up and down, becoming very aggressive to anyone who approaches. Will hiss as if to display displeasure. The adults molt primary flight feathers while raising their young, rendering family groups flightless at the same time. Several subspecies vary geographically around the U.S. Generally they are paler in color in eastern groups, and darker in western. Size decreases northward, with the smallest subspecies found on the Arctic tundra.

SANDHILL CRANE
Grus canadensis

YEAR-ROUND
MIGRATION
WINTER

Size:	40-48" (102-120 cm); up to 7-foot wingspan
Male:	Elegant gray bird with long legs and neck. Wings and body often stained rusty brown. Scarlet red cap. Red eyes.
Female:	same as male
Juvenile:	dull brown without red cap, yellow eyes
Nest:	platform, on the ground; female and male build; 1 brood per year
Eggs:	2; olive with brown markings
Incubation:	28-32 days; female and male incubate
Fledging:	65 days; female and male feed young
Migration:	complete, to southern states and Mexico, winters in southern half of Florida
Food:	insects, fruit, worms, plants, amphibians
Compare:	Similar size as Great Blue Heron (pg. 265), but Heron flies with its neck in an S shape, unlike Crane's straight neck. Larger than Tricolored Heron (pg. 95), but lacks blue head and wings, and white undersides.

Stan's Notes: Among the tallest birds in the world and capable of flying at great heights. Usually seen in large undisturbed fields near water. Often heard before seen, they have a very distinctive rattling call. Plumage often appears rust brown because of staining from mud during preening. Characteristic flight with upstroke quicker than down. For their spectacular mating dance the performers face each other, bow and jump into the air while uttering a loud cackling sound and flapping wings. Often flips sticks and grass into the air during dance.

GREAT BLUE HERON
Ardea herodias

YEAR-ROUND

Size: 42-52" (107-132 cm)

Male: Tall gray heron. Black eyebrows extend into several long plumes off the back of head. Long yellow bill. Feathers at base of neck drop down in a kind of necklace.

Female: same as male

Juvenile: same as adult, but more brown than gray, with a black crown and no plumes

Nest: platform; male and female build; 1 brood per year

Eggs: 3-5; blue green, unmarked

Incubation: 27-28 days; female and male incubate

Fledging: 56-60 days; male and female feed young

Migration: complete, to southern states, Central and South America, winters in Florida

Food: small fish, frogs, insects, snakes

Compare: Tricolored Heron (pg. 95) is half the size with a white belly. Similar size as Sandhill Crane (pg. 263), but lacks the Crane's red crown. Crane flies with neck held straight, unlike the Heron's S-shaped neck.

Stan's Notes: One of the most common herons, it often barks like a dog when startled. Seen stalking small fish in shallow water. Will strike at mice, squirrels and just about anything else it might come across. Flies holding neck in an S shape, with its long legs trailing straight out behind. The wings are held in cupped fashion during flight. Nests in colonies of up to 100 birds. Nests in treetops near or over open water.

male

female

RUBY-THROATED HUMMINGBIRD
Archilochus colubris

SUMMER
WINTER

Size: 3-3½" (7.5-9 cm)

Male: Tiny iridescent green bird with black throat patch that reflects bright ruby red in sun.

Female: same as male, lacking throat patch

Juvenile: same as female

Nest: cup; female builds; 1-2 broods per year

Eggs: 2; white, unmarked

Incubation: 12-14 days; female incubates

Fledging: 14-18 days; female feeds young

Migration: complete, to southern states, Mexico and Central America

Food: nectar, insects

Compare: No other bird is as tiny. The Sphinx Moth hovers at flowers like the Hummingbird, but has clear wings and a mouth part that looks like a straw, which coils up when not at a flower. Moves much slower than the Hummingbird and can be approached.

Stan's Notes: The smallest bird in the state. Able to hover, fly up and down, and is the only bird to fly backward. Does not sing, but will chatter or buzz to communicate. The wings create a humming noise, flapping 50 to 60 times per second or faster during chasing flights. Weighing just 2 to 3 grams, it takes about five average-sized hummingbirds to equal the weight of a single chickadee. The heart beats at an incredible 1,260 times a minute and it breathes 250 times a minute. Constructs its nest with plant material and spider webs, gluing pieces of lichen on the outside of nest for camouflage. Attracted to tubular red flowers.

male

female

PAINTED BUNTING
Passerina ciris

MIGRATION
SUMMER
WINTER

Size: 5½" (14 cm)

Male: An amazing combination of colors. A green back, deep blue head, and an orange chest and belly with dark wings and tail.

Female: bright green above and light green below

Juvenile: drab version of the female with only some small spots of green

Nest: cup; the female and male build; 1-2 broods per year

Eggs: 3-5; pale blue with brown markings

Incubation: 11-12 days; female incubate

Fledging: 12-14 days; female and male feed young

Migration: complete, to southern states, the Bahamas, Cuba, Mexico and Central America

Food: seeds, insects, will visit seed feeders

Compare: No other bird can compare with the male's striking colors. Female is uniquely green and rarely confused with any other bird.

Stan's Notes: A wonderful bird of backyard gardens, woodland edges and along brushy roads, it will visit seed feeders in wooded yards. Well known for its loud, clear and varied warbling phrases. Cup nest, made of grass and lined with animal hair, is often in a deep, tangled mass of vines. A common cowbird host, which usually unfortunately results in raising only the cowbird young and not its own. Although it winters in the southern half of Florida, most continue migrating and leave the state. More well known in Texas and Oklahoma. Often captured in Central America and sold as a caged bird, which is not legal in North America.

YEAR-ROUND

MONK PARAKEET
Myiopsitta monachus

Size: 12" (30 cm)

Male: A lime green back and belly. Gray forehead extending into chest. Tips and trailing edge of wings are blue. A short, hooked yellow bill. Long narrow tail.

Female: same as male

Juvenile: same as adult

Nest: cavity, in large stick nest; female and male build; 1 brood per year

Eggs: 4-6; off-white without markings

Incubation: 12-14 days; female incubates

Fledging: 28-30 days; female and male feed young

Migration: non-migrator

Food: fruit, seeds

Compare: Several parakeet species occur in Florida, but the Monk Parakeet is the most widespread in southern Florida. Usually seen in urban parks.

Stan's Notes: Unlike other birds, the Monk Parakeet has two toes forward and two pointing back, compared with three forward and only one back. The toe arrangement helps the foot hold food while bringing it to the mouth. Huge colony nest is made of sticks. There are over 300 parakeet species in the world. The Monk Parakeet, originally from Argentina, now breeds in southern Florida. The only native North American parakeet was the Carolina Parakeet, last reported in Florida in the 1920s and now extinct. All parakeets currently in Florida came from release or are escaped pets.

male

female pg. 181

WOOD DUCK
Aix sponsa

Size: 17-20" (43-50 cm)

Male: A small, highly ornamented dabbling duck with a green head and crest patterned with white and black. A rusty chest, white belly and red eyes.

Female: brown, similar size and shape to male, has bright white eye ring and a not-so-obvious crest, blue patch on wing often hidden

Juvenile: same as female

Nest: cavity; female lines old woodpecker cavity; 1 brood per year

Eggs: 10-15; creamy white, unmarked

Incubation: 28-36 days; female incubates

Fledging: 56-68 days; female teaches young to feed

Migration: complete, to southern states, non-migrator in Florida

Food: aquatic insects, plants, seeds

Compare: Smaller than the male Northern Shoveler (pg. 277). Lacks Shoveler's long wide bill.

Stan's Notes: A common duck of quiet, shallow backwater ponds. Nearly extinct around 1900 due to over-hunting, but is doing well now. Nests in old woodpecker holes or nest boxes. Often seen flying deep in forest or perched high up in trees. Female takes flight with loud squealing call and enters nest cavity from full flight. Will lay eggs in a neighboring female nest (egg dumping), resulting in some clutches in excess of 20 eggs. Young remain in nest cavity only 24 hours after hatching, then jump from up to 30 feet to the ground or water to follow their mother, never returning to the nest.

GREEN HERON
Butorides virescens

YEAR-ROUND
SUMMER

Size: 16-22" (40-56 cm)

Male: Short stocky heron with a blue-green back, and rusty red neck and chest. Dark green crest. Short legs, normally yellow, but turn bright orange during breeding season.

Female: same as male

Juvenile: similar to adult, with a blue-gray back and white-streaked chest and neck

Nest: platform; female and male build; 2 broods per year

Eggs: 2-4; light green, unmarked

Incubation: 21-25 days; female and male incubate

Fledging: 35-36 days; female and male feed young

Migration: complete, to South America, winters in most of Florida

Food: fish, insects, aquatic plants

Compare: Green Heron is smaller than the Tricolored Heron (pg. 95) and lacks the long neck of most other herons. Look for a small heron with a dark green back stalking wetlands.

Stan's Notes: Often gives an explosive, rasping "skyew" call when startled. Sometimes it looks like it doesn't have a neck, because it holds its head close to its body. Hunts for fish and aquatic insects by waiting along a shore or wades stealthily. Has been known to place an object, such as an insect, on the water surface to attract fish to catch. Has a crest that it raises when excited.

male

female pg. 183

WINTER

NORTHERN SHOVELER
Anas clypeata

Size: 20" (50 cm)

Male: Medium-sized duck with iridescent green head, rusty sides and white breast. Has an extraordinarily large spoon-shaped bill that is almost always held pointed toward water.

Female: same spoon-shaped bill, brown and black all over and blue wing patch

Juvenile: same as female

Nest: ground; female builds; 1 brood per year

Eggs: 9-12; olive, unmarked

Incubation: 22-25 days; female incubates

Fledging: 30-60 days; female leads young to food

Migration: complete, to southern states and Central America, winters in Florida

Food: aquatic insects, plants

Compare: Similar to the male Mallard (pg. 281), but Shoveler has a large, characteristic spoon-shaped bill. Larger than the average male Wood Duck (pg. 273) and lacks the Wood Duck's crest.

Stan's Notes: One of several species of shoveler, so called because of the peculiarly shaped bill. The Northern Shoveler is the only species of these ducks in North America. A winter visitor, it arrives in Florida in September and leaves in April. Seen in small flocks of five to ten, swimming low in water with large bills always pointed toward the water, as if they're too heavy to lift. Feeds primarily by filtering tiny plants and insects from the water's surface with bill.

female pg. 195

male

RED-BREASTED MERGANSER
Mergus serrator

WINTER

Size: 23" (58 cm)

Male: A shaggy green head and crest. Prominent white collar. Black and white body. A long orange bill.

Female: overall brown to gray with a reddish head and crest, long orange bill

Juvenile: similar to adult, male looks like the female at first, then changes

Nest: ground; female builds; 1 brood per year

Eggs: 5-10; olive green without markings

Incubation: 29-30 days; female incubates

Fledging: 55-65 days; female feeds young

Migration: complete, to the southern coastal states and Central America, winters in coastal Florida

Food: fish, aquatic insects

Compare: Larger than the male Hooded Merganser (pg. 55), which has a large white patch on head, compared with the green head of the male Red-breasted Merganser.

Stan's Notes: A winter resident of coastal Florida. It is the most common of the wintering mergansers, arriving in late October and leaving in April. Most commonly seen along both coasts, but can also be seen in large inland freshwater lakes. A very fast flyer, often seen flying low and fast across the water. Needs a long take-off run to get airborne. Serrated bill helps it catch slippery fish. Doesn't breed before 2 years of age. Males abandon females just after eggs are laid. Females often share a nest. Nests across northern Canada and Alaska.

female pg. 199

male

YEAR-ROUND

MALLARD
Anas platyrhynchos

Size: 27-28" (69-71 cm)

Male: Large, bulbous green head, white necklace and rust brown or chestnut-colored chest. A combination of gray and white on sides. Yellow bill, legs and feet.

Female: all brown with orange and black bill, small blue and white wing mark (speculum)

Juvenile: same as female, but with yellow bill

Nest: ground; female builds; 1 brood per year

Eggs: 7-10; greenish to whitish, unmarked

Incubation: 26-30 days; female incubates

Fledging: 42-52 days; female leads young to food

Migration: complete, to southern states, non-migrator in Florida

Food: seeds, plants, aquatic insects, will come to ground feeders offering corn

Compare: The male Northern Shoveler (pg. 277) has a white chest with rust on sides and dark spoon-shaped bill.

Stan's Notes: A familiar duck of lakes and ponds. Will return to place of birth. The name "Mallard" comes from the Latin *masculus*, meaning "male," referring to the habit of males not taking part in raising ducklings. Both male and female have white tails and white underwings. Black central tail feathers of male curl upward.

male

female pg. 321

MIGRATION
WINTER

AMERICAN REDSTART
Setophaga ruticilla

Size: 5" (13 cm)

Male: Small, striking black bird with contrasting patches of orange on sides, wings and tail. White belly.

Female: olive brown with yellow patches instead of the male's orange, white belly

Juvenile: same as female, the juvenile male is tinged orange for first year

Nest: cup; female builds; 1 brood per year

Eggs: 3-5; off-white with brown markings

Incubation: 12 days; female incubates

Fledging: 9 days; female and male feed young

Migration: complete, to Florida, Mexico, Central and South America

Food: insects, seeds, berries rarely

Compare: Male Red-winged Blackbird (pg. 9) and the male Baltimore Oriole (pg. 285) are much larger at roughly 8 inches. The only small black and orange bird flitting around tops of trees.

Stan's Notes: A common, widespread warbler in the state during migration and the winter. Prefers large unbroken tracts of forest. Appears hyperactive when feeding, hovering and darting back and forth to glean insects from the leaves. Look for flashing black and orange color high in the trees. Often droops its wings and fans its tail just before launching out to catch an insect.

male

female pg. 329

BALTIMORE ORIOLE
Icterus galbula

MIGRATION
WINTER

Size: 7-8" (18-20 cm)

Male: Bright flaming-orange bird with black head and black extending down nape of neck onto the back. Black wings with white and orange wing bars. An orange tail with black streaks. Gray bill and dark eyes.

Female: pale yellow with orange tones, gray brown wings, white wing bars, gray bill, dark eyes

Juvenile: same as female

Nest: pendulous; female builds; 1 brood per year

Eggs: 4-5; bluish with brown markings

Incubation: 12-14 days; female incubates

Fledging: 12-14 days; female and male feed young

Migration: complete, to Florida, Mexico, Central and South America

Food: insects, fruit, nectar, comes to orange half and nectar feeders

Compare: The male Orchard Oriole (pg. 287) is much darker orange than the Baltimore's flaming orange. Male American Redstart (pg. 283) is smaller and has more black than orange.

Stan's Notes: A fantastic songster, this bird is often heard before seen. Easily attracted to a feeder offering grape jelly, orange halves or sugar water (nectar). Parents bring young to feeders. Sits in tops of trees feeding on caterpillars. Female builds sock-like nest at the outermost branches of tall trees. Often returns to the same area year after year. Usually seen during migration and winter.

female pg. 331

male

ORCHARD ORIOLE
Icterus spurius

SUMMER

Size: 7-8" (18-20 cm)

Male: Dull orange bird with black head and black extending down the back. A black chin, tail and wings. Single white wing bars. A long, thin black bill with a small gray mark on lower mandible (jaw).

Female: olive green back with dull yellow belly, two white wing bars on dark gray wings

Juvenile: same as female, first-year male has a black bib

Nest: pendulous; female builds; 1 brood per year

Eggs: 3-5; pale blue to white, brown markings

Incubation: 11-12 days; female and male incubate

Fledging: 11-14 days; female and male feed young

Migration: complete, to central Mexico and northern South America

Food: insects, fruit, comes to fruit/nectar feeders

Compare: Similar to male Baltimore Oriole (pg. 285), but the male Orchard Oriole has a much darker orange body.

Stan's Notes: A summer resident in the northern part of Florida. Prefers orchards and open woods, hence its common name. Eats insects until wild fruit starts to ripen. It usually nests alone, but sometimes in small colonies. Parents bring the young to jelly and orange half feeders shortly after fledging. Many people mistakenly think the orioles have left during the summer but, in fact, the birds are concentrating on finding insects to feed their young.

female pg. 101

male

YEAR-ROUND

HOUSE FINCH
Carpodacus mexicanus

Size: 5" (13 cm)

Male: An orange red face, chest and rump, with brown cap. Brown marking behind eyes. Brown wings streaked with white. A white belly with brown streaks.

Female: brown with heavily streaked white chest

Juvenile: similar to female

Nest: cup, sometimes in cavities; female builds; 2 broods per year

Eggs: 4-5; pale blue, lightly marked

Incubation: 12-14 days; female incubates

Fledging: 15-19 days; female and male feed young

Migration: non-migrator to partial migrator, will move around to find food

Food: seeds, fruit, leaf buds, will visit seed feeders

Compare: Male Purple Finch (pg. 291) is very similar, but male House Finch lacks the red cap. Look for the streaked chest and belly, and brown cap of male House Finch.

Stan's Notes: The House Finch was originally introduced to Long Island, New York, in the 1940s from western America. A very social bird, it visits feeders in small flocks. Seems to prefer nesting in hanging flower baskets. Incubating female is fed by male. Loud and cheerful warbling song. Suffers from a fatal eye disease that causes the eyes to crust over.

female pg. 111

male

PURPLE FINCH
Carpodacus purpureus

WINTER

Size:	6" (15 cm)
Male:	Raspberry-red head, cap, breast, back and rump. Brownish wings and tail.
Female:	heavily streaked brown and white bird with large white eyebrows
Juvenile:	same as female
Nest:	cup; female and male build; 1 brood a year
Eggs:	4-5; greenish blue with brown markings
Incubation:	12-13 days; female incubates
Fledging:	13-14 days; female and male feed young
Migration:	irruptive, moves around in search of food
Food:	seeds, insects, fruit, comes to seed feeders
Compare:	Redder than the orange red of male House Finch (pg. 289), with a clear (no streaking) red breast. The male House Finch has a brown cap, compared with the male Purple Finch's red cap.

Stan's Notes: Usually only seen during winter in northern Florida, when flocks of Purple Finches leave their homes farther north and move around looking for food. Travels in flocks of up to 50. Comes to seed feeders along with House Finches, making it hard to tell them apart. A rich loud song and a distinctive "tic" note is made only in flight. Not a purple color, the Latin name *purpureus* means "crimson" or other reddish color.

female
pg. 333

male

SUMMER TANAGER
Piranga rubra

YEAR-ROUND
SUMMER
WINTER

Size: 8" (20 cm)

Male: Bright rosy-red bird with darker red wings.

Female: overall yellow with slightly darker wings

Juvenile: male has patches of red and green over the entire body, female is same as adult female

Nest: cup; female builds; 1-2 broods per year

Eggs: 3-5; pale blue with dark markings

Incubation: 10-12 days; female incubates

Fledging: unknown days; female and male feed young

Migration: complete, to Central and South America

Food: insects, fruit

Compare: Similar size as the male Northern Cardinal (pg. 295), but Cardinal has a black mask, large crest and red bill.

Stan's Notes: A distinctive bird of Florida's woodland, especially in mixed pine and oak forest. Due to the clearing of land for agriculture, populations have been decreasing over the past century, especially during the last two decades. Returning to Florida in late March and with young hatching in May, some have two broods per year. Most leave the state by November with very few remaining for winter. While fruit makes up some of the diet, most of it consists of insects such as bees and wasps. Summer Tanagers unfortunately seem to be parasitized by Brown-headed Cowbirds more than just about any other nesting bird in Florida.

female pg. 133

male

YEAR-ROUND

NORTHERN CARDINAL
Cardinalis cardinalis

Size: 8-9" (20-22.5 cm)

Male: All-red bird with a black mask extending from face down to chin and throat. Large red bill and crest.

Female: buff brown with tinges of red on crest and wings, same black mask and red bill

Juvenile: same as female, with blackish gray bill

Nest: cup; female builds; 2-3 broods per year

Eggs: 3-4; bluish white with brown markings

Incubation: 12-13 days; female and male incubate

Fledging: 9-10 days; female and male feed young

Migration: non-migrator

Food: seeds, insects, fruit, comes to seed feeders

Compare: Similar size as the male Summer Tanager (pg. 293), but Tanager is a rosy red. Look for Northern Cardinal's black mask, large crest and red bill.

Stan's Notes: A familiar backyard bird. Look for the male feeding female during courtship. Male feeds young of the first brood by himself while female builds second nest. The name comes from the Latin word *cardinalis*, which means "important." Very territorial in spring, it will fight its own reflection in a window. Non-territorial during winter, gathering in small flocks of up to 20 birds. Both the male and female sing, and can be heard anytime of year. Listen for its "whata-cheer-cheer-cheer" territorial call in spring.

juvenile

ROSEATE SPOONBILL
Ajaia ajaja

YEAR-ROUND
WINTER

Size: 32" (80 cm); up to 4-foot wingspan

Male: An overall pink bird with red highlights. A white neck with a black patch on the back of the head. A heavy, spoon-shaped flat bill. Long red legs.

Female: same as male

Juvenile: pale version of adult

Nest: platform; female and male build; 1 brood per year

Eggs: 1-4; olive green with dark markings

Incubation: 22-23 days; male and female incubate

Fledging: 35-42 days; female and male feed young

Migration: partial migrator to non-migrator

Food: fish, aquatic insects, snails, worms, leeches

Compare: An unmistakable bird of Florida, Spoonbill is larger than White Ibis (pg. 315), which has a long, down-curved orange-to-red bill unlike the heavy flat bill of the Spoonbill.

Stan's Notes: A coastal resident of Florida. Is making a comeback from devastating hunting pressures in the 1800s for wing feathers that were used in women's hats and fans. Now habitat destruction is limiting their numbers. Swings its spoon-shaped bill to sift fish and aquatic insects from shallow waters. Usually found in small flocks. Nests in mixed colonies with herons.

in flight

LEAST TERN
Sterna antillarum

Size: 9" (22.5 cm)

Male: A white and gray tern with black cap, white forehead and light-orange-yellow bill with a dark tip. White belly. Legs are same color as the bill. Black wing tips and a short, deeply forked tail, seen in flight.

Female: same as male

Juvenile: browner version of adult, has dark bill and partial black cap during first summer

Nest: ground; female builds; 1 brood per year

Eggs: 1-3; olive green with dark markings

Incubation: 20-22 days; female incubates

Fledging: 19-20 days; female teaches young to feed

Migration: complete, to South America

Food: aquatic insects, fish

Compare: Half the size of Royal Tern (pg. 307), which has black legs and a large orange-red bill, unlike Least's smaller, light-orange-yellow bill with a dark tip. In flight, look for black wing tips and a short, deeply forked tail.

Stan's Notes: The smallest tern in North America, the Least Tern is also an endangered species in many North American locations. Killed by the hundreds of thousands in the early 1900s for its feathers, its decreasing numbers are now due to predators, such as cats and dogs, and human disturbance while nesting. Nests in large colonies on sandy beaches. Will often hover over intruders in the colony. Hunts small fish and aquatic insects by plunging into water or skimming over the surface. Recognizes mate by distinctive calls.

WINTER

FORSTER'S TERN
Sterna forsteri

Size: 14-15" (36-38 cm)

Male: A white and gray tern with jet black crown, and an orange bill with a black tip. Leading edge of wings is gray, trailing edge is white. Characteristic forked tail is long and white. Winter plumage lacks black crown and bill becomes nearly entirely black.

Female: same as male

Juvenile: similar to adult, minus the black crown

Nest: platform; female and male build; 1 brood per year

Eggs: 3-5; tan to white with brown markings

Incubation: 23-24 days; female and male incubate

Fledging: 24-26 days; male and female feed young

Migration: complete, to Central America, winters in Florida

Food: small fish, aquatic insects

Compare: Smaller than Royal Tern (pg. 307), which has larger orange-red bill. Look for jet black crown, orange bill with black tip and white tips of wings. The Least Tern (pg. 299) is smaller and has a light-orange-yellow bill.

Stan's Notes: Usually seen in small colonies. Catches small fish by diving into the water headfirst. Will catch insects in flight. Builds a platform nest on floating vegetation. Nests in small colonies in shallow-water marshes. Named after Johann Reinhold Forster, a German naturalist who accompanied Captain Cook around the world in 1772.

winter

breeding

YEAR-ROUND
WINTER

LAUGHING GULL
Larus atricilla

Size: 16-17" (40-43 cm); up to 3⅓-foot wingspan

Male: Breeding adult has black head "hood," and white neck, chest and belly. Slate gray back and wings with black wing tips, and orange bill. Winter plumage lacks the "hood" and has a black bill.

Female: same as male

Juvenile: brown throughout, gray sides, lacking the black head and white chest, gray bill

Nest: ground; the male and female build; 1 brood per year

Eggs: 2-4; olive with brown markings

Incubation: 18-20 days; female and male incubate

Fledging: 30-35 days; male and female feed young

Migration: complete, East and Gulf coasts, Central and South America, winters in southern Florida

Food: fish, insects, aquatic insects

Compare: Smaller than the Ring-billed Gull (pg. 305) and Herring Gull (pg. 313). Look for black head "hood," and slate gray back and wings of Laughing Gull.

Stan's Notes: A "three-year" gull, Laughing Gull starts out mostly brown and gray. Second year it resembles the adult version, but lacks complete black head "hood." Third year is breeding plumage. Nests in marshes in large colonies. Male tosses his head back and calls to attract a mate. Nest is a scrape on ground lined with grass, sticks and rocks. Young fed a half-digested regurgitant by adults.

winter

juvenile

breeding

RING-BILLED GULL
Larus delawarensis

WINTER

Size: 19" (48 cm)

Male: A white bird with gray wings, black wing tips spotted with white, and a white tail, as seen in flight. Yellow bill with a black ring near tip. Yellowish legs and feet.

Female: same as male

Juvenile: mostly gray version of adult, has dark band at end of tail

Nest: ground; the female and male build; 1 brood per year

Eggs: 2-4; off-white with brown markings

Incubation: 20-21 days; female and male incubate

Fledging: 20-40 days; female and male feed young

Migration: complete, to southern states and Mexico, winters in Florida

Food: insects, fish, scavenges

Compare: Similar to Herring Gull (pg. 313), which has an orange mark on tip of lower bill. Herring Gull has pink legs and feet, and lacks Ring-billed Gull's black ring.

Stan's Notes: A common gull of garbage dumps and parking lots. It is expanding its range and remains farther north longer during winter due to successful scavenging in cities. Acquires a new and different plumage in each of the first three autumns and doesn't attain adult plumage until the third year. Attains ring on bill after the first winter.

winter

in flight

breeding

ROYAL TERN
Sterna maxima

YEAR-ROUND
WINTER

Size: 20" (50 cm)

Male: Black legs and feet. A large orange-red bill. Gray back and gray upper surface of wings with white below. Tail is forked. Breeding has a black cap extending down the nape. Winter has a white forehead and only a partial black cap.

Female: same as male

Juvenile: dull white to gray with only a hint of black cap rarely extending down nape

Nest: ground; female and male build; 1-2 broods per year

Eggs: 1-2; off-white with dark brown markings

Incubation: 30-31 days; female and male incubate

Fledging: 28-35 days; female and male feed young

Migration: complete, to Central and South American coasts, winters in coastal Florida

Food: fish, aquatic insects

Compare: Larger than Forster's Tern (pg. 301), which has a small black-tipped bill. Twice the size of Least Tern (pg. 299), which has a light-orange-yellow bill and a shorter forked tail.

Stan's Notes: A winter resident in coastal Florida. It nests in large colonies on islands in the Banana River and Tampa Bay, and other places in southern coastal Florida. Lays a single egg in a shallow depression on the ground. Like other terns, the Royal Tern plunges from heights of 40 feet and more into water headfirst to capture fish and aquatic insects.

CATTLE EGRET
Bubulcus ibis

Size: 20" (50 cm)

Male: All-white and stocky. Disproportional large round head. Yellow bill and legs. Breeding adult has an orange buff crest, breast and back with red-orange bill and legs.

Female: same as male

Juvenile: similar to adult, but has red-orange bill and legs of breeding adult

Nest: platform; female and male build; 1 brood per year

Eggs: 2-5; light blue green without markings

Incubation: 22-26 days; female and male incubate

Fledging: 28-30 days; female and male feed young

Migration: partial migrator, to southern states, Central and South America, moves to find food

Food: insects, small mammals

Compare: About half the size of Great Egret (pg. 317), which has a much longer neck, black legs and a much larger bill. White Ibis (pg. 315) has a long orange-to-red down-curved bill.

Stan's Notes: Came to South America from Africa around 1880, reaching Florida in the 1940s. Often seen singularly in pastures, hunting insects at cow and horse pies. Holding its head still while wiggling its neck back and forth and from side to side, it stabs at prey, captures it, then tosses it to the back of its mouth in one swift move. Often attracted to field fires to hunt newly exposed animals and insects. Breeds in large colonies of up to 1,000 or more pairs. In some years it is found as far as northern tier states and Canada.

SNOWY EGRET
Egretta thula

YEAR-ROUND
SUMMER

Size: 24" (60 cm)

Male: All-white bird with black bill and legs, and bright yellow feet. Long feather plumes on the head, neck and back during breeding season.

Female: same as male

Juvenile: similar to adult, but backs of legs are yellow

Nest: platform; female and male build; 1 brood per year

Eggs: 3-5; light blue-green, unmarked

Incubation: 20-24 days; female and male incubate

Fledging: 28-30 days; female and male feed young

Migration: complete, Gulf coast and Mexico, winters in most of Florida

Food: aquatic insects, fish

Compare: Much smaller than Great Egret (pg. 317), which has black feet and yellow bill. Same size as juvenile Little Blue Heron (pg. 93), which has a black-tipped gray bill.

Stan's Notes: Common in wetlands and often seen with other egrets, colonies may include up to several hundred nests. Nests are low in shrubs 5 to 10 feet tall or are on the ground, usually mixed among other egret and heron nests. Chicks hatch days apart (asynchronous), leading to starvation of the last to hatch. Will actively "hunt" prey by moving around quickly, stirring up small fish and aquatic insects with its feet. In the breeding state, a yellow patch at base of the bill and yellow feet turn orange-red. Was hunted to near extinction in the late 1800s for its feathers.

breeding

winter

WINTER

HERRING GULL
Larus argentatus

Size: 23-26" (58-66 cm)

Male: Common "sea gull" of large lakes. A snow-white bird with slate gray wings and black wing tips with tiny white spots. Yellow bill with red spot near tip of lower mandible. Pinkish legs.

Female: same as male

Juvenile: uniformly mottled brown to gray, black bill

Nest: ground; the female and male build; 1 brood per year

Eggs: 2-3; olive with brown markings

Incubation: 24-28 days; female and male incubate

Fledging: 35-36 days; female and male feed young

Migration: complete, to coasts that remain unfrozen in North America, winters in Florida

Food: fish, insects, clams, eggs, baby birds

Compare: Larger than the Ring-billed Gull (pg. 305), which has a black ring around its bill and lacks orange dot on lower mandible. Ring-billed Gull has yellow legs, compared with the Herring Gull's pinkish legs.

Stan's Notes: An opportunistic bird, scavenging food from dumpsters, but will also take other birds' eggs and young right from nest. Often drops clams and other shellfish from heights to break shells and get to the soft interior. Nests in colonies, returning to same site year after year. Lines nest with grasses and seaweed. Adults molt to a dirty gray in winter, looking similar to juveniles. Takes about four years for juveniles to obtain adult plumage.

juvenile

WHITE IBIS
Eudocimus albus

Size: 25" (63 cm); up to 3-foot wingspan

Male: All-white bird with a very long, downward-curved orange-to-red bill. Pink facial skin. Leg color matches the bill. Black wing tips, seen only in flight.

Female: same as male, but smaller and with less of a down-curved bill

Juvenile: combination of chocolate brown and white for the first two years, dull orange bill

Nest: platform; female and male build; 1 brood per year

Eggs: 2-3; light blue with dark markings

Incubation: 21-23 days; female and male incubate

Fledging: 28-35 days; female and male feed young

Migration: partial migrator to non-migrator in Florida

Food: aquatic insects, crustaceans, fish

Compare: One of two native ibis in Florida, the long down-curved bill helps identify them. The White Ibis is all white and is not confused with the brown Glossy Ibis (pg. 193).

Stan's Notes: More common in southern Florida. It prefers fresh water over salt water, with crayfish being a big part of the diet. A white bird with black wing tips and a bright orange-to-red down-curved bill make this bird easy to identify. Often seen flying in groups of 30 or more. Nests in large colonies in well-made stick nests. The non-native all-red Scarlet Ibis (not shown), which was introduced in the 1960s, often hybridizes with the White Ibis and produces young in various shades of pink or red.

GREAT EGRET
Ardea alba

YEAR-ROUND
MIGRATION

Size: 38" (96 cm)

Male: Tall, thin, elegant all-white bird with long, pointed yellow bill. Black stilt-like legs and black feet.

Female: same as male

Juvenile: same as adult

Nest: platform; male and female build; 1 brood per year

Eggs: 2-3; light blue, unmarked

Incubation: 23-26 days; female and male incubate

Fledging: 43-49 days; female and male feed young

Migration: complete, to southern states, Mexico and Central America, winters in most of Florida

Food: fish, aquatic insects, frogs, crayfish

Compare: The Snowy Egret (pg. 311) is much smaller with yellow feet and a black bill vs. Great Egret's black feet and yellow bill. Almost twice the size of the Cattle Egret (pg. 317), which has a much shorter neck and smaller bill. Larger than juvenile Little Blue Heron (pg. 93), which has a black-tipped gray bill.

Stan's Notes: A tall and stately bird, the Great Egret slowly stalks shallow wetlands looking for small fish to spear with its long sharp bill. Nests in colonies of up to 100 birds. Now protected, they were hunted to near extinction in the 1800s and early 1900s for their long white plumage. The name "Egret" came from the French word *aigrette*, which means "ornamental tufts of plumes." The plumes are grown near the tail during breeding season.

chick-feeding
adult

AMERICAN WHITE PELICAN
Pelecanus erythrorhynchos

MIGRATION
WINTER

Size: 62" (158 cm); up to 9-foot wingspan

Male: A large white bird with black wing tips that extend partially down the trailing edge of wings. A white or pale yellow crown. Bright yellow bill, legs and feet. Breeding adult has a bright orange bill and legs. An adult that is feeding chicks (chick-feeding adult) has a gray-black crown.

Female: same as male

Juvenile: duller white with brownish head and neck

Nest: ground; a scraped-out depression, rimmed with dirt; 1 brood per year

Eggs: 1-3; white without markings

Incubation: 29-36 days; male and female incubate

Fledging: 60-70 days; female and male feed young

Migration: complete, to Central and South America

Food: fish

Compare: Very similar to the Brown Pelican (pg. 203), only white with a bright yellow or orange bill. Look for black wing tips in flight.

Stan's Notes: Often seen in large groups on larger lakes. American White Pelicans feed by simultaneously dipping their bills into the water to scoop up fish. They don't dive into water to catch fish, like coastal Brown Pelicans. Bills and legs of breeding adults turn deep orange. Breeding adults also usually grow a flat fibrous plate in the middle of the upper mandible. The plate drops off after eggs have hatched. They fly in a large V, often gliding with long wings, then all flapping together.

male pg. 283

female

AMERICAN REDSTART
Setophaga ruticilla

Size: 5" (13 cm)

Female: Olive brown with yellow patches on sides, wings and tail. White belly.

Male: small, striking black bird with contrasting patches of orange on sides, wings and tail, white belly

Juvenile: same as female, the juvenile male is tinged orange for first year

Nest: cup; female builds; 1 brood per year

Eggs: 3-5; off-white with brown markings

Incubation: 12 days; female incubates

Fledging: 9 days; female and male feed young

Migration: complete, to Florida, Mexico, Central and South America

Food: insects, seeds, berries rarely

Compare: Similar to female Yellow-rumped Warbler (pg. 211), but lacking the Warbler's yellow patch on rump.

Stan's Notes: A common, widespread warbler in the state during migration and the winter. Prefers large unbroken tracts of forest. Appears hyperactive when feeding, hovering and darting back and forth to glean insects from the leaves. Look for flashing black and orange color high in the trees. Often droops its wings and fans its tail just before launching out to catch an insect.

male

winter male

female

WINTER

AMERICAN GOLDFINCH
Carduelis tristis

Size: 5" (13 cm)

Male: A perky yellow bird with a black patch on forehead. Black tail with conspicuous white rump. Black wings with white wing bars. No marking on the chest. Dramatic change in color during winter, similar to female.

Female: dull olive yellow without a black forehead, brown black wings and white rump

Juvenile: same as female

Nest: cup; female builds; 1 brood per year

Eggs: 4-6; pale blue, unmarked

Incubation: 10-12 days; female incubates

Fledging: 11-17 days; female and male feed young

Migration: partial migrator, flocks of up to 20 move around North America

Food: seeds, insects, will come to seed feeders

Compare: Is confused with other winter birds. Female Purple Finch (pg. 111) has heavily streaked chest and white line above eyes. The female House Finch (pg. 101) has heavily streaked white chest.

Stan's Notes: Most often found in open fields, scrubby areas and in woodland. Often called Wild Canary. A feeder bird that enjoys Nyger Thistle. Late summer nesting, uses the silky down from wild thistle for its nest. Appears roller-coaster-like in flight. Listen for it to twitter during flight. Almost always in small flocks. Moves into Florida for winter starting in November. Can be a common visitor to feeders all winter, leaving in April for northern states.

COMMON YELLOWTHROAT
Geothlypis trichas

YEAR-ROUND

Size: 5" (13 cm)

Male: Olive brown bird with bright yellow throat and breast, a white belly and a distinctive black mask outlined in white. A long, thin, pointed black bill.

Female: same as male, only lacking black mask

Juvenile: same as female

Nest: cup; female builds; 2 broods per year

Eggs: 3-5; white with brown markings

Incubation: 11-12 days; female incubates

Fledging: 10-11 days; female and male feed young

Migration: complete, to southern states and Central America, winters in Florida

Food: insects

Compare: Found in a similar habitat as the American Goldfinch (pg. 323), but lacks the male's black forehead and wings. Yellow-rumped Warbler (pg. 211) only has spots of yellow, compared with Yellowthroat's yellow breast.

Stan's Notes: A common warbler of open fields and marshes. Has a cheerful, well-known song, "witchity-witchity-witchity-witchity." The male performs a curious courtship display, bouncing in and out of tall grass while uttering an unusual song. The young remain dependent upon the parents longer than most warblers. A frequent cowbird host.

WINTER

PALM WARBLER
Dendroica palmarum

Size: 5½" (14 cm)

Male: Distinctive yellow eyebrows. Yellow throat, belly and undertail. An obvious chestnut-colored crown. On the sides of breast, thin chestnut-colored streaks. A dark line across dark eyes.

Female: same as male

Juvenile: same as adult, but duller and brown

Nest: cup; female builds; 1-2 broods per year

Eggs: 4-5; white with brown markings

Incubation: 11-12 days; female incubates

Fledging: 12-13 days; female and male feed young

Migration: complete, to Florida, the West Indies and Central America

Food: insects, fruit

Compare: Similar size as the Yellow-rumped Warbler (pg. 211), but the Yellow-rumped lacks a yellow throat and belly. Look for the yellow eyebrows and chestnut-colored crown.

Stan's Notes: One of the most common and abundant winter warblers, the more common being the Yellow-rumped Warbler. Often seen in backyard woodland during winter. Look for it to wag or bob its tail while gleaning bugs from leaves and flowers of trees. One of the few warblers that feeds on the ground. Hops rather than walks. Nests at edge of northern spruce bogs. Recognizes cowbird eggs and will destroy the eggs by burying them with a new nest built right over the top of the old nest.

male pg. 285

female

BALTIMORE ORIOLE
Icterus galbula

MIGRATION
WINTER

Size: 7-8" (18-20 cm)

Female: A pale yellow bird with orange tones, gray brown wings, white wing bars, a gray bill and dark eyes.

Male: bright flaming-orange bird with black head and black extending down nape of neck onto the back, black wings with white and orange wing bars, an orange tail with black streaks, gray bill and dark eyes

Juvenile: same as female

Nest: pendulous; female builds; 1 brood per year

Eggs: 4-5; bluish with brown markings

Incubation: 12-14 days; female incubates

Fledging: 12-14 days; female and male feed young

Migration: complete, to Florida, Mexico, Central and South America

Food: insects, fruit, nectar, comes to orange half and nectar feeders

Compare: Very similar to the female Orchard Oriole (pg. 331), which lacks orange tones and has less pronounced wing bars.

Stan's Notes: A fantastic songster, this bird is often heard before seen. Easily attracted to a feeder offering grape jelly, orange halves or sugar water (nectar). Parents bring young to feeders. Sits in tops of trees feeding on caterpillars. Female builds sock-like nest at the outermost branches of tall trees. Often returns to the same area year after year. Usually seen during migration and winter.

male pg. 287

female

ORCHARD ORIOLE
Icterus spurius

SUMMER

Size: 7-8" (18-20 cm)

Female: An olive green bird with a dull yellow belly. Two white wing bars on dark gray wings. Long, thin black bill with a small gray mark on lower mandible (jaw).

Male: dull orange with a black head, chin, upper back, wings and tail, single white wing bars

Juvenile: same as female, first-year male has a black bib

Nest: pendulous; female builds; 1 brood per year

Eggs: 3-5; pale blue to white, brown markings

Incubation: 11-12 days; female and male incubate

Fledging: 11-14 days; female and male feed young

Migration: complete, to central Mexico and northern South America

Food: insects, fruit, comes to fruit/nectar feeders

Compare: Similar to female Baltimore Oriole (pg. 329), which has orange overtones and more pronounced wing bars. The female Summer Tanager (pg. 333) is mustard yellow with a larger, thicker bill.

Stan's Notes: A summer resident in the northern part of Florida. Prefers orchards and open woods, hence its common name. Eats insects until wild fruit starts to ripen. It usually nests alone, but sometimes in small colonies. Parents bring the young to jelly and orange half feeders shortly after fledging. Many people mistakenly think the orioles have left during the summer but, in fact, the birds are concentrating on finding insects to feed their young.

male pg. 293

female

SUMMER TANAGER
Piranga rubra

YEAR-ROUND
SUMMER
WINTER

Size: 8" (20 cm)

Female: Some show a faint wash of red, but most females are a mustard yellow overall with slightly darker wings.

Male: bright rosy-red bird with darker red wings

Juvenile: male has patches of red and green over the entire body, female is same as adult female

Nest: cup; female builds; 1-2 broods per year

Eggs: 3-5; pale blue with dark markings

Incubation: 10-12 days; female incubates

Fledging: unknown days; female and male feed young

Migration: complete, to Central and South America

Food: insects, fruit

Compare: Similar to female Orchard Oriole (pg. 331) and Baltimore Oriole (pg. 329). The female Summer Tanager lacks wing bars and has a larger bill.

Stan's Notes: A distinctive bird of Florida's woodland, especially in mixed pine and oak forest. Due to the clearing of land for agriculture, populations have been decreasing over the past century, especially during the last two decades. Returning to Florida in late March and with young hatching in May, some have two broods per year. Most leave the state by November with very few remaining for winter. While fruit makes up some of the diet, most of it consists of insects such as bees and wasps. Summer Tanagers unfortunately seem to be parasitized by Brown-headed Cowbirds more than just about any other nesting bird in Florida.

EASTERN MEADOWLARK
Sturnella magna

YEAR-ROUND

Size: 9" (22.5 cm)

Male: A robin-shaped bird with a brown back, a lemon-yellow chest and prominent black V-shaped necklace. White outer tail feathers.

Female: same as male

Juvenile: same as adult

Nest: cup, on the ground in dense cover; female builds; 2 broods per year

Eggs: 3-5; white with brown markings

Incubation: 13-15 days; female incubates

Fledging: 11-12 days; female and male feed young

Migration: complete, to Central America, winters in Florida

Food: insects, seeds

Compare: The only large yellow bird with a black V mark on chest.

Stan's Notes: A bird of open grassy country. Best known for its wonderful song. Often seen perched on a fence post, it will quickly dive into tall grass if approached. Has conspicuous white markings on each side of its tail, most often seen when flying away. Nest is sometimes domed with dried grass. Named "Meadowlark" because it's a bird of meadows and sings like the larks of Europe. Eastern Meadowlark's song is a flute-like, clear whistle. Not a member of the lark family, it actually belongs to the blackbird family. Related to grackles and orioles.

Helpful Resources:

Bird Behavior, Vol I, II, III. Stokes, Donald and Lillian Stokes. Boston: Little, Brown and Company, 1989.

Birder's Bug Book, The. Waldbauer, Gilbert. Cambridge: Harvard University Press, 19

Birder's Dictionary. Cox, Randall T. Helena, MT: Falcon Press Publishing, 1996.

Birder's Handbook, The. Ehrlich, Paul, David S. Dobkin and Darryl Wheye. New York: Simon and Schuster, 1988.

Birds Do It, Too: The Amazing Sex Life of Birds. Harrison, George and Kit Harrison. Minocqua, WI: Willow Creek Press, 1997.

Birds of Forest, Yard, and Thicket. Eastman, John. Mechanicsburg, PA: Stackpole Books, 1997.

Birds of North America. Kaufman, Kenn. New York: Houghton Mifflin, 2000.

Blackbirds of the Americas. Orians, Gordon. Seattle: University of Washington Press, n.d.

Bluebird Book, The. Stokes, Donald and Lillian Stokes. Boston: Little, Brown and Company, 1991.

Cry of the Sandhill Crane, The. Grooms, Steve. Minocqua, WI: Northword Press, 1992.

Dictionary of American Bird Names, The. Choate, Ernest A. Boston: Harvard Common Press, 1985.

Everything You Never Learned About Birds. Rupp, Rebecca. Pownal, VT: Storey Publishing, 1995.

Field Guide to the Birds East of the Rockies, A. Peterson, Roger Tory. Boston: Houghton Mifflin, 1980.

Field Guide to the Birds of North America, Third Edition. Washington, DC: National Geographic Society, 1999.

Field Guide to Warblers of North America, A. Dunn, Jon and Kimball Garrett. Boston: Houghton Mifflin, 1997.

Florida's Birds: A Handbook and Reference. Kale, Herbert, W., II and David S. Maehr. Sarasota: Pineapple Press, 1990.

Florida Birds Species: An Annotated List, Special Publication No. 6. Robertson, William B., Jr. and Glen E. Woolfenden. n.p.: Florida Ornithological Society, 1992.

Folklore of Birds. Martin, Laura C. Old Saybrook, CT: Globe Pequot Press, 1993.

How Birds Migrate. Kerlinger, Paul. Mechanicsburg, PA: Stackpole Books, 1995.

Lives of Birds, Birds of the World and Their Behavior, The. Short, Lester L. New York: Henry Holt and Company, 1993.

Lives of North American Birds. Kaufman, Kenn. Boston: Houghton Mifflin, 1996.

Living on the Wind. Weidensaul, Scott. New York: North Point Press, 1999.

National Audubon Society: North American Birdfeeder Handbook. Burton, Robert. New York: Dorling Kindersley Publishing, 1995.

National Audubon Society: The Sibley Guide to Birds. Sibley, David Allen. New York: Alfred A. Knopf, 2000.

Photographic Guide to North American Raptors, A. Wheeler, Brian K. and William S. Clark. New York: Academic Press, 1995.

Secret Lives of Birds, The. Gingras, Pierre. Toronto: Key Porter Books, 1997.

Secrets of the Nest. Dunning, Joan. Boston: Houghton Mifflin, 1994.

Sparrows and Buntings. Byers, Clive, Jon Curson and Urban Olsson. New York: Houghton Mifflin, 1995.

Stokes Field Guide to Birds: Eastern Region. Stokes, Donald and Lillian Stokes. Boston: Little, Brown and Company, 1996.

Stokes Purple Martin Book. Stokes, Donald and Lillian Stokes. Boston: Little, Brown and Company, 1997.

Florida Birding Hotlines. For reporting unusual bird sightings or to hear a recording of where birds have been seen, call these prerecorded hotlines:

Florida Rare Bird Alert Statewide
561-340-0079

Lower Keys Rare Bird Alert
305-294-3438

Northwest Florida Rare Bird Alert
850-934-6974

Miami Rare Bird Alert
305-667-7337

North Florida Rare Bird Alert
912-244-9190

WEB PAGES:

The Internet has become a valuable place to learn about birds. The following are a few web sites that will assist you in your pursuit of birds. You might find birding on the net a fun way to learn more about birds or to spend a long winter night.

SITE	ADDRESS
Audubon of Florida	www.audubon.usf.edu
Florida Ornithological Society	www.flmnh.ufl.edu/fos
American Birding Association	www.americanbirding.org
Cornell Lab of Ornithology	www.birds.cornell.edu
Author Stan Tekiela's home page	www.naturesmart.com

CHECK LIST/INDEX

Use the boxes to check the birds you've seen.

ABOUT THE AUTHOR:

Stan Tekiela is a naturalist, author and wildlife photographer with a Bachelor of Science degree in Natural History from the University of Minnesota. He has been a professional naturalist for nearly 20 years and is a member of the Minnesota Naturalist Association. Stan actively studies and photographs birds throughout the United States. He received an Excellence in Interpretation award from the National Association for Interpretation, and a regional award for Commitment to Outdoor Education. A columnist and radio personality, his syndicated column appears in more than 20 cities and he can be heard on a number of radio stations. Stan resides in Victoria, Minnesota, with wife Katherine and daughter Abigail. He can be contacted via his web page at www.naturesmart.com.

OTHER BOOKS BY STAN TEKIELA:

Birds of the Carolinas Field Guide
Birds of New Jersey Field Guide
Birds of New York Field Guide
Birds of Connecticut Field Guide
Birds of Massachusetts Field Guide
Nature Smart: A Family Guide to Nature
Start Mushrooming: The Easiest Way to Collect Edible Mushrooms
Plantworks: 15 Common Edible Plants